THE
VAMPIRE
COMBAT
MANUAL

THE VAMPIRE COMBAT MANUAL

A Guide to Fighting the Bloodthirsty Undead

ROGER MA

ILLUSTRATIONS BY KURT MILLER

BERKLEY BOOKS, NEW YORK

THE BERKLEY PUBLISHING GROUP
Published by the Penguin Group
Penguin Group (USA) Inc.
375 Hudson Street, New York, New York 10014, USA
Penguin Group (Canada), 90 Eglinton Avenue East, Suite 700, Toronto, Ontario M4P 2Y3, Canada
(a division of Pearson Penguin Canada Inc.)
Penguin Books Ltd., 80 Strand, London WC2R 0RL, England
Penguin Group Ireland, 25 St. Stephen's Green, Dublin 2, Ireland (a division of Penguin Books Ltd.)
Penguin Group (Australia), 250 Camberwell Road, Camberwell, Victoria 3124, Australia
(a division of Pearson Australia Group Pty. Ltd.)
Penguin Books India Pvt. Ltd., 11 Community Centre, Panchsheel Park, New Delhi—110 017, India
Penguin Group (NZ), 67 Apollo Drive, Rosedale, Auckland 0632, New Zealand
(a division of Pearson New Zealand Ltd.)
Penguin Books (South Africa) (Pty.) Ltd., 24 Sturdee Avenue, Rosebank, Johannesburg 2196,
South Africa

Penguin Books Ltd., Registered Offices: 80 Strand, London WC2R 0RL, England

This book is an original publication of The Berkley Publishing Group.

Copyright © 2012 by Roger Ma.
Cover design by Diana Kolsky.
Cover illustrations and Vampire Combat Club logo by Kurt Miller.
Interior illustrations by Kurt Miller.
Text design by Georgia Rucker.

PUBLISHING HISTORY
Berkley trade paperback edition / October 2012

Library of Congress Cataloging-in-Publication Data

Ma, Roger.
The vampire combat manual : a guide to fighting the bloodthirsty undead / Roger Ma.
    p. cm.
ISBN 978-0-425-24765-5
1. Vampires. I. Title.
GR830.V3M17 2012
398.21—dc23
        2012011585

PRINTED IN THE UNITED STATES OF AMERICA

10 9 8 7 6 5 4 3 2 1

Most Berkley Books are available at special quantity discounts for bulk purchases for sales promotions, premiums, fund-raising, or educational use. Special books, or book excerpts, can also be created to fit specific needs. For details, write: Special Markets, The Berkley Publishing Group, 375 Hudson Street, New York, New York 10014.

To Zoe, Logan, and Jonas, who will never have to fear the night

CONTENTS

II. Anatomy 19

III. Conditioning and Preparation 71

IV. Weapons 121

V. Combat Strategies and Techniques 163

VI. Team-Based Combat 251

WARNING

The conditioning routines, nutritional recommendations, and fighting techniques contained within this manual are meant to maximize your effectiveness in combat, specifically against the vampire species. Proceed with caution with the information provided, and always consult your physician before commencing any type of training regimen, particularly ones designed to protect you from the undead.

INTRODUCTION

You are being hunted. Maybe not today, or this month. Perhaps not even this year. If you plan on living an existence outside of your primary residence once the sun sinks past the horizon, however, it is likely that you will be the target of a predator far more powerful than yourself. Since the dawn of civilization, the human race has taken solace in its perception of being at the apex of the ecological pyramid: the dominant species on planet Earth. Sadly, this is not the case. Most of the general populace is unaware of the fact that another species has usurped our position of supremacy. *Sanguinem potantes,* "drinkers of blood," otherwise known as the vampire. Unfortunately for us, these creatures are as effective as we are at hunting species lower on the food chain.

The original intent of this text was quite simple. As an investigative researcher, I was contracted by IUCS, a global bioresearch firm with whom I have worked in the past, to explore and document the efforts of the Blood Assassins, an organization renowned as much for its secrecy as for its skill in neutralizing the vampire threat. My objective was to locate and interview willing members, detail their motivations, and chronicle their unique approach toward this adversary for the public. Should you be one of my funding patrons reading this work solely based upon that initial premise, allow me to save you the time and report that, in regard to my previously stated objective, I have been unsuccessful.

As in many quests, however, the journey often proves more valuable than the destination. In my efforts to complete this assignment, I have discovered a stark reality: Our existence on this planet rests on delicate threads, far more fragile and tenuous than ever imagined. I have also uncovered a global threat that, left unchecked, may cause the downfall of humanity as we know it. It was imperative to me that, despite being unable to track down this specific organization, I provide the everyday citizen with the combative information gleaned from my research in order to survive a vampire attack.

Throughout this investigative journey, I have also learned that the greatest enemy of knowledge is not ignorance, but misinformation. An ignorant individual can improve upon his lack of knowledge; a misinformed one acts upon and spreads misinformation to others, often with tragic consequences. In daily life, these inaccuracies may result in embarrassment, awkwardness, or slight humiliation. In vampire combat, these falsehoods can result in injury, death, or, as I've learned, a fate much worse. The research conducted and techniques provided in this manual have a singular purpose: to draw back the curtain on decades of propaganda and focus a light on the proper methods to survive an undead attack with your blood supply intact.

This work, however, is not intended to be a treatise that transforms you into a self-styled "vampire hunter." Hunting, by definition, is conducted by creatures higher on the food chain, targeting prey that is smaller, weaker, and more vulnerable to attack. In comparison to vampires, Homo sapiens fall into the latter class. Only those with the highest degree of skill, experience—or stupidity—would willingly seek out these encounters.

Why then create such a manual, if not to take the fight to the enemy? During a vampire attack, most individuals will face off against a stronger, faster, and more agile opponent. Firearms are largely ineffective against this particular adversary. Long-range weaponry requires a high degree of skill possessed by only a select few. Thus, there is no question that when confronted by a vampire, you *will* be engaging in hand-to-hand combat. If you want to survive while sustaining minimal injury, you have no other choice but to fight back. Without the proper strategy and techniques, it is virtually impossible to survive a vampire's onslaught. Why create such a manual? To help you endure.

You will also find within these pages interviews conducted with members of the very species I am providing you the understanding with which to destroy. It is only through my unique and obscure network of contacts that I was able to obtain access to these beings. What I had hoped to discover through these interactions was insight into the behavior and patterns of those who hunt us by night. At great personal risk, I fought to bring these voices to light. The result of my efforts, I am the first to admit, are inconclusive. As I learned in my research, the vampire species conducts both a physical and a mental battle against its prey. Even for someone in my line of work, someone who is used to being deceived, it was difficult to discern lies from the truth. There were times when I felt manipulated, influenced, and coerced into purposely detailing my exchanges with these creatures. I believe, however, that there was enough accuracy in their words to warrant full disclosure, which I have provided to you within these pages. However, I caution the reader against taking their words completely at face value. If I have learned anything from this journey, it is that engaging in vampire combat is as much a psychological battle as it is a physical one.

The other significant finding I have discovered is that, despite the inherent physical disadvantages we as humans face against this cunning and powerful adversary, the situation is far from dire. In fact, a combatant trained in the tactics of countering a vampire attack has a high likelihood of success. These are the tactics I will share with you in the pages that follow.

A vampire may not be the type of opponent you can overpower or outrun, but with proper instruction, a well-planned strategy, and a little luck, this is an opponent you can outfight.

I.

DISINFORMATION AND MISCONCEPTIONS

All war is deception.

— SUN TZU

Their history spans centuries. Their reputation, steeped in mystery. Their legend transcends cultures and traverses continents. Vlad the Impaler, Nosferatu, Count Dracula: historic and mythical representations for the species known to modern society as the vampire. As with many creatures with such a long and storied past, many varied accounts exist of their traits, behaviors, and exploits. Most of these tales are no more than fables—sinister yarns told by adults in order to coax obedience from misbehaving children. As a result, much confusion exists between vampire fact and vampire fiction.

Through the research conducted for this text, we have discovered that many of the falsehoods that exist regarding this species are not only untrue, they continue to be perpetuated by those who stand to benefit the most from their acceptance: the vampire species itself. This organized campaign of disinformation enables these myths to spread in perpetuity, continually gaining acceptance and maintaining a seductive mystique around the species. Due to these rampant inaccuracies, it is imperative that we review in detail the most common misconceptions regarding this parasitic creature, focusing on those myths that can have a direct impact on combat with a member of the undead.

Before we embark on deciphering these misconceptions, we must clarify some terminology you will encounter throughout this work. We use several different monikers to describe our opponent: succubus, ghoul, vampire, the undead. While the nomenclature may change, the fundamental taxonomy remains the same: a nocturnal creature that hunts human beings for the sole purpose of draining their blood for its own sustenance.

MISCONCEPTION #1:
VAMPIRES ARE METAPHYSICAL BEINGS

Of all the falsehoods that exist regarding the vampire, this single misconception has caused more human deaths than all others combined. It is a natural inclination to believe a being that must travel in darkness, is helpless against sunlight, and drinks the blood of living beings in order to survive is demonic in nature—one summoned by the underworld to wreak havoc on Earth—and can be weakened by the powers of the sacred or the pious. Unfortunately, this is far from the truth.

A myriad of analyses that have been conducted regarding this misconception have shown that the transformation from Homo sapiens into a member of the vampire species is strictly secular in nature, and has no connection to any particular religious or divine beliefs. Those who rely on any faith-related talismans to counter a vampire's onslaught will find their opponent completely unfazed. Countless stories abound of individuals trusting these methods to assist them in their encounter with the undead to their own detriment. Here is but one example:

> Several people went missing from our small village, a woman and two young children. The police said it was the work of vagrants or bandits, but we all knew better. After two more went missing, my friend Eduardo and I took it upon ourselves to rid us of this menace. We were two of the strongest men in our village, and spent a month's worth of daylight searching the town and the neighboring valley. Finally, after weeks of exploration, we found its lair embedded in one of the many hillside caves surrounding the countryside.

I. DISINFORMATION AND MISCONCEPTIONS

Armed with flasks of holy water and two large wooden crucifixes blessed by the village priest, we approached the creature's den a few hours before sunset. We found a large, heavy crate deep within its dwelling. As I lifted the lid, Eduardo opened one of the flasks and doused the creature's face with the blessed liquid. It did not cause the reaction we had hoped.

The creature rose from its crate, dabbed the water from its face, and smashed the flask atop Eduardo's skull. With shards of glass embedded in his forehead and blood running down his face, Eduardo turned to me with a look of disbelief and horror. I raised one of the crosses directly into the creature's face, hoping it would reel back in fear. It laughed terribly, grabbed the crucifix, and snapped it in two. It then took the jagged end of the cross and thrust it into Eduardo's shoulder. He screamed in pain. I was near paralyzed with fright. It grabbed Eduardo, and before it came for me, I scurried out of the lair and ran back to the village, collapsing in an exhausted heap on my bed.

When I awoke the next morning, I nearly believed I had imagined the entire previous day. Then I heard a sound at my front door: a muffled, plaintive cry, as if coming from a wounded animal. When I opened my door, a large burlap sack sat on my doorstep. I pulled it into my home and cautiously opened it. Inside was Eduardo. He had been turned. All four of his limbs had also been severed at the joints. Eduardo looked into my eyes and, with his newly forming canines gnashing in his mouth, kept repeating the same phrase: *"Matar a mí, por favor. Matar a mí."* I took the bag into my yard and let the sun turn him into dust. My family and I packed our belongings and left the country that same day, before the sun had set.

—*Francisco, Baeza, Spain*

To ascertain the validity of this misconception, IUCS analysts conducted their own comprehensive study. It remains to this day one of the few research studies that involved an actual confined member of the vampire species (how the subject was obtained for the study still remains confidential). The research initiative was entitled "Project Deity."

Leaders representing various religious sects, including Judaism, Islam, Buddhism, and Christianity, were invited to confront the creature with whatever charms, amulets, and writings they believed would assist their efforts. No time limit was placed on the interaction, the only requirement being that no physical contact could be used as part of their interaction with the participant. The results of the project were, in the analysts' words, "tragic."

None of the representatives, regardless of origin of faith or artifact used, were successful in causing the slightest negative reaction in the participant. Worse still, two of the clergy renounced their faith entirely after extensive discourse with the subject; another assisted in the escape of the participant by sacrificing his own body to feed the subject, who regained the strength to neutralize the security personnel monitoring the session and successfully fled the research facility.

MISCONCEPTION #2:
VAMPIRES ARE SHAPESHIFTERS

Another popular belief, reinforced by depictions in popular culture, is that vampires are able to alter their physical structure to mimic other nocturnal creatures—wolves, rodents, and, most notably, bats. Some also believe that the creature can morph into climatological apparitions such as mist, smoke, or fog. Neither is true. Were any of these the case, there would be nothing preventing such a creature from converting into one of these entities the moment its survival was in jeopardy. As you will learn during our discussion of anatomy, a vampire, while possessing a heightened set of physical characteristics, is still tethered by the limitations of the humanoid corporal form. This limitation is the creature's greatest weakness, and a critical factor in our ability to overcome this undead threat. Vampires are not able to change into other mammalian creatures, nor can they transform into vapor. They do, however, seem to possess some skill in manipulating the behaviors of these lower order creatures, which may have given rise to the rumor that the species is capable of mutating into these life-forms.

MISCONCEPTION #3:
VAMPIRES CAN FLY

Another myth propagated by the species is that vampires, like the nocturnal mammals with which they are most frequently associated, can take flight or levitate at will. Despite the legend, no anatomical alteration occurs during the transformation of human into vampire that would enable the creature to glide, fly, or hover in the air, nor can they scuttle up the sides of sheer wall faces like arachnids. The only reasonable explanation why this is believed is that perhaps witnesses saw a vampire launch an attack on a victim by dropping down from an aerial position, or the creature's athleticism enabled it to leap across structures and obstacles that normal humans would have difficulty traversing, both providing the illusion of flight. Regardless of what you have heard or seen, vampires are unable to fly, even if wearing garments that would facilitate such an act.

MISCONCEPTION #4:
VAMPIRES ARE SEXUALLY ATTRACTED TO HUMANS

One of the most pervasive and insidious misconceptions of the vampire, second only to the idea that it is supernatural, is that it is a highly sexualized being, one capable of and interested in fornicating with the human species. Charming, sexy, erotic—these are common adjectives often used to describe the undead. The myth of the vampire as a titillating imp is as old as the creature itself, and with good reason. Through a deliberate and proactive crusade on the part of the species, this association has been allowed to develop in all forms of media. This disinformation has grown so accepted that there is a huge population of humans who lust after members of the species—precisely what this campaign of disinformation hoped to achieve. The truth of the matter is much different. Human beings engage in sexual intercourse with other humans for two reasons: pleasure or procreation. Let us address each of these directly when speaking in terms of the undead. In regard to pleasure, a vampire derives no physical satisfaction from copulating with a human victim. In fact, it is rumored that the genitalia of the vampire cease to function as they would in their human state, although this has not been corroborated by any certified laboratory examination. As far as procreation is concerned, although vampires are also capable of propagating their kind, they do so through very different means (see Misconception #5).

Some may wonder why creatures with such an effective ability to track and hunt prey would bother to vociferously promote such a misconception. Although the vampire's hunting prowess does enable it to secure victims with relative ease, there is always an inherent risk of injury every time the creature must feed. A simpler prospect is to have willing participants who offer no resistance in the hope of experiencing the intimacy they have been convinced exists. As you will read later in this work, this tactic has been used to great effectiveness by a specific sect within the vampire species. No hostility, no conflict, a simple and efficient meal. By embracing the myth of the provocative, sultry bloodsucker, many have played directly into the creatures' hands. As far as attraction to the human species is concerned, vampires are no more physically enticed to their prey than humans can be attracted to their evening meal.

MISCONCEPTION #5:
VAMPIRE INFECTION IS INEVITABLE

As mentioned previously, the vampire's ability to propagate its species is markedly different from the method of procreation performed by Homo sapiens. The means by which these creatures multiply is via direct contact through their masticatory system, specifically the vampire bite. As a result, it is commonly believed that once a vampire has buried its fangs into your flesh, you will by default become a member of the undead, having been "infected" by its wound. While automatic conversion may be true for other types of undead creatures, it is not the case with the vampire.

The confusion surrounding the conversion process is largely a result of misinterpreting the transmission of the transforming agent itself. It was previously believed the biological agent that turns a human being into the bloodthirsty undead operates similar to a pathogen or retrovirus, transferred at the moment of salivary contact between the *vector*, the carrier of the agent, and its victim. In actuality, the transmission is comparable to the mating practices of certain invertebrates, such as Turbellaria (flatworms), Strepsiptera (twisted-winged parasites), and Cimicidae, commonly known as bedbugs, which coincidentally also feed upon human blood. Creatures such as these impregnate by means of "traumatic insemination," whereby one partner causes a laceration on the other partner's torso and ejaculates into the open wound. Interestingly, this method of transmission among these invertebrates is not limited to male/female couples nor to members of the same species—similar to the vampire's method of conversion.

Through traumatic insemination, a vampire is able to deliberately infuse a victim with the bacterium that transforms human beings into members of the undead. Although the specific chemical matrix has not yet been isolated, research has determined that these compounds are released into the victim's bloodstream during the feeding session to launch this turning process.

The vampire's motivation for initiating the conversion sequence is entirely subjective. In other words, it is the creature that decides who will or will not become a member of its species, with the vast majority of victims not selected for conversion. The vampire's complete decision criteria for species selection is, as of this writing, unknown. The assessment may have to do with physical features, characteristics, or a specific skill set possessed by the human target. Outside of this hypothesized rationale, the judgment to convert a human victim is yet undetermined.

Hopefully you can take solace in the fact that should you suffer a vampire's bite in combat, you will not necessarily be doomed to an undead existence.

MISCONCEPTION #6:
VAMPIRES ARE INDESTRUCTIBLE

Another common myth that exists concerning the vampire is that it is virtually impossible to defeat in battle, and exerting any type of defensive technique against an attacking succubus is an effort in futility. This is exactly what the species would like you to believe. It is easy to think that creatures with such a long and formidable, if not always accurate, history are completely invulnerable to any threat posed by a normal human opponent.

It is the case that vampires are resilient organisms boasting a wide array of physiological strengths. Many conventional methods of neutralizing a human opponent will not apply in undead combat, and to use them would certainly mean your defeat. There are, however, significant and available vulnerabilities that, once exploited, make surviving a confrontation with a vampire not only possible, but very likely depending on your level of knowledge and training. The knowledge follows in these pages. The training is in your hands.

MISCONCEPTION #7: VAMPIRES LOVE BEING UNDEAD

"Sleep All Day. Party All Night. Never Grow Old. Never Die." In eleven words, this tag line from a popular eighties film summarized the appealing elements humans associate with the undead lifestyle. As there is a great deal of accuracy in the slogan, what is so negative about being a vampire? The truth is, a considerable amount. Although there are many aspects that humans may find appealing to being a member of this particular species, the reality is far from the perception. While it is true that some vampires fully embrace their new existence and will actively recruit others to join their ranks, the majority of converted humans experience tremendous negativity and depression in their new, undead lives. Loss of familial ties, unrelenting bloodlust, and the lack of exposure to sunlight all contribute to a literal and figurative dark existence for these creatures. Upward of 20 percent of the world-wide vampire population commit self-annihilation on an annual basis, typically via exposure to ultraviolet light. It is the reason the overall vampire population, despite conversions continually taking place and the species as a whole never succumbing to human means of death, has remained constant for hundreds of years.

• • •

Having reviewed all the above misconceptions, it may come as a surprise to you that many of the vampire traits that you believed to be true, perhaps since childhood, are in fact false. How is it possible then that these myths are believed by such a large majority of the population? This is the very definition of disinformation—falsehoods that are intentionally spread with the purpose of confusing the general public, often to generate fear and insecurity. The species has been very effective in orchestrating this campaign of confusion within the human populace. Let the deceptions end with this text.

COMBAT REPORT: JASON RICHTER

Vampire
Chicago, Illinois

I pass through an unmarked doorway from an alleyway on Smith Street, the entrance to a speakeasy nearly a century old. There are many saloons in Chicago that create a false air of menace, hoping to attract young, attractive professionals looking for a pseudo-sinister place to imbibe. This is not one of those places. During the Prohibition era, it was rumored that this establishment was renowned for drawing the most notorious of clientele. From the looks of the current patrons, it seems not much has changed. No one acknowledges my presence, nor that of Heinrick, my bodyguard. Given my interview subject, I took it upon myself to hire professional security as a precautionary measure. A former member of the Dutch Special Forces and a K1 heavyweight kickboxing contender, Heinrick steps slightly in front of me and presses his

*beefy palm against my chest as he scans the room for immediate
threats. Satisfied, we proceed to the back of the bar as instructed.*

*Seated at a table against the rear wall is Jason Richter, vampire.
From outward appearances, Mr. Richter looks completely mundane.
Nothing in his manner, dress, or appearance provides even a slight
hint of his background. Pudgy and balding, he could easily be mistaken for a run-of-the-mill businessman, which I learn was exactly
his profession prior to his conversion. Richter offers me the seat opposite him. He too does not acknowledge Heinrick, who stands close by.*

Vampire Combat Manual: Do you remember anything about
your conversion?
Jason Richter: July seventh, 1981.

VCM: You remember the exact date?
JR: We all do. As natural as remembering your own birthday,
which, ironically enough, I have forgotten.

I was the senior comptroller for a midsize insurance company in Seattle. The financial quarter had just ended, and I
was trying to catch up after the July Fourth holiday break.
Since Karen, my daughter, was going to her first sleepover
that evening, my wife only had to deal with Mark, our tod-
dler, which gave me the excuse to work late that night. Not
that I needed an excuse. Julie was a very trusting woman.
Even with our two young children, she accepted the fact that
I had to put in the hours, often coming home long after the
house was fast asleep. I didn't see much of her for a while, or
the kids, or anyone else for that matter except my coworkers.
And Marguerite.

*Richter shifts forward in his chair, causing Heinrick to jump to at-
tention. Richter glances at him briefly before shifting back in his seat.*

JR: Marguerite—Margy—was one of the cleaning women in
our office. I saw her often on those late nights. We struck up

a friendship. She seemed shy at first, just a "hello" and "thank you" when I would hand her my trash pail, but I believed she appreciated the acknowledgment. Most of the staff was gone by the time she started her shift, and those that were around ignored her. By the time I left in the evenings, it was often just the two of us on the floor.

After a while, we started speaking more as friends. She shared stories about her family, and I told her about my life as a late-blooming father. She was curious about what I did for a living and expressed interest in going back to school, although she mentioned that she was embarrassed of her thick Spanish accent. I was more than happy to help her understand what exactly I did as comptroller. After months of those talks, she probably had a better idea of what I did at work than most people at the company.

Richter shifts again, seemingly uncomfortable in his chair. He rubs the back of his neck with a pained sense of urgency. He seems to settle down and continues to speak.

JR: I was working late again one night, and didn't see Margy making her rounds. I figured she called in sick or had the night off. At about 3 a.m, I was in the restroom rinsing my face, trying to keep myself awake. I turned from the sink to dry my eyes, and there she stood, staring at me. I smiled and asked if she couldn't at least knock first. Margy didn't laugh. After a few awkward seconds, I tried to move past her when she gripped my forearm. I remember the pain being excruciating. She grabbed me by the throat with her other hand, and forced me backward effortlessly. We both crashed through the bathroom stall door as she began to press her fingers against my throat. I started to push and flail against her, trying to free myself when Margy smiled, and said, in perfect English, "This will be much easier if you don't resist, Jason." My world went black, forever. That was July seventh, 1981.

Richter seems troubled again. He grips the edge of the table with both hands and slowly exhales. He reaches into his jacket lapel pocket, which causes a defensive stir in Heinrick. Richter removes a small plastic bag filled with a maroon-colored fluid. It takes me only a moment to identify the contents. He rips open the top of the package, and empties the contents down his throat. He tosses the empty container on the table. Richter's agitation seems to subside, and he is able to continue.

JR: I woke several hours later, still in the bathroom stall. My head was resting against the base of the toilet, but I couldn't feel the cold of the porcelain. I did feel the thirst. "Thirst" is a bit inaccurate. You don't feel it only in your mouth or throat. You feel it in the very depths of your bones. I would say you feel it in your *soul*, if that term wasn't completely ludicrous to me at this point. I made my way out of the office, and instinctively headed for home. When I arrived at my doorstep and heard Julie's footsteps coming down the staircase as I rang the bell, I could smell the blood coursing through her veins. She opened the door. Julie was a very trusting woman. She didn't resist. Neither did Mark.

VCM: Did you ever learn why you were turned?
JR: The reasons no longer matter. They once did, I guess, but I've since stopped caring. In the days following my turning, I discovered that Margy was very thorough. These were the days before computerized record keeping and redundant backup systems. The informal education I provided to her made it easy to make it appear as if I absconded with a sizable portion of my company's payroll. The official story is that I murdered my wife and son after misappropriating millions from my employer, and disappeared into the ether. Why the elaborate setup, I'm still not exactly certain; it's not as if I was going to show up at the precinct to declare my innocence.

VCM: A vampire existence is often portrayed as an enjoyable one. What has been your experience?

Richter remains silent for several minutes. The stillness becomes awkward, and I clear my throat to ask a different question, but he begins to speak.

JR: Imagine having to disconnect yourself from every person you have ever loved: your parents, your spouse, your friends, your children, knowing that should you ever encounter them again, your only thought would be how fast you could drain their bodies. Imagine the worst physical pain you have ever experienced in your life: a shattered bone, a mind-numbing migraine, a debilitating illness. Imagine experiencing that pain replicated in every cell of your body, as if you could feel every one of the millions of nuclei splintering and bursting in agony. Now imagine experiencing that feeling every few days without adequate nourishment. That is what I must endure for an eternity. I've heard "experts" likening our feeding to the needs of a drug addict. It is much worse. There is no feeling of euphoria, no jubilation, no joy in satiating the thirst. There is only momentary relief, as if pouring water into a sack with a rip at the bottom; the minute you've topped off, the need to replenish it is almost immediate. How enjoyable does that sound?

I've answered enough of your questions. I would appreciate you fulfilling our agreement.

I hand Richter a sealed envelope. Within it are photographs taken several weeks earlier, when I met with Karen Richter, the daughter who spent that evening decades earlier at a friend's home. Now in her mid-thirties, Karen was taken in by her mother's grandparents after the events described by my subject. I met with her under the guise of being a journalist researching unsolved criminal cases. Most of the photos are of Karen herself. Some are with her children.

Richter removes the photos and stares at each for what seems an eternity, as if trying to will emotions long forgotten. His face remains expressionless, and he quietly replaces the photos in the envelope.

VCM: Are you familiar with a group known as the Blood Assassins?

In an instant, Richter seems to transform before my eyes. He opens his mouth obscenely wide and hisses, all the humanity seemingly drained from him. He leaps over to my side of the table. Heinrick pushes me aside and draws his firearm. Richter grabs Heinrick's gun hand by the wrist and twists his arm hideously backward, the opposite direction it is meant to move. The muscles and tendons in his rotator cuff snap like packing tape. Before Heinrick has an opportunity to cry out in pain, Richter snatches the pistol from his hand and strikes him across the temple, knocking him unconscious. None of the bar patrons react. Richter stands and adjusts his attire.

JR: A word of advice if you want to live to see the completion of your work. Do not mention that group again should you meet with others of my kind. Most will not receive it as thoughtfully as I have. And in the future, save your money on the thug and get yourself something more useful.

Before I can ask for an explanation, Richter departs. On the table lies the envelope containing the photos of his daughter, next to the empty blood packet. I retrieve both items, along with Heinrick, and depart the speakeasy. No one acknowledges our exit.

I. DISINFORMATION AND MISCONCEPTIONS

II.

ANATOMY

This war differs from other wars...We are not fighting armies but a hostile people, and must make old and young, rich and poor, feel the hard hand of war.

—WILLIAM TECUMSEH SHERMAN

Found on every continent and every human-inhabited landmass on the planet, a vampire will often adopt the dress, mannerisms, and cultural subtleties representative of its host nation. Despite these superficial differences, the fundamental biology of the creature appears to remain consistent across cultures and societies. Detailed knowledge of the vampire's anatomical structure is limited, as a full-scale vivisection of the creature has never been conducted; much about the vampire still remains a scientific mystery. However, enough information has been anecdotally confirmed to make ourselves a viable threat to the creature's defenses. Since the intention of this work is to provide practical combative data rather than deep medical analysis, we will focus our anatomical discussion on details that have specific ramifications in a hostile engagement with a member of the vampire species.

LIVING OR DEAD?

Due to the vampire's similarities to the Homo sapiens life-form, scholars and religious leaders often have difficulty classifying whether the creature is living or dead. While the metaphysical argument can be debated ad nauseam, a scientific assessment of the creature's physiology makes the issue much clearer. Unlike a human being's, the vampire's physical structure does not process oxygen; nor does it require any external nutrients other than one: *sanguinem mortalem*, human blood. In the strictest sense of the word, a vampire is not a living creature. At the same time, the fact that the creature is ambulatory, requires rest and recuperation, and does exhibit many human qualities calls into question whether it is "dead." For lack of a better term, many researchers have come to refer to vampires as the "undead," beings that, while not exhibiting physical characteristics that we would define as living, are also not deceased. Throughout this text, we have also co-opted this terminology to describe these particular creatures.

While this argument may seem semantic in nature, it does serve an important purpose in our discussion. It is easy for humans to anthropomorphize these beings; to wish that they are still just like us. In fact, it is precisely this mentality that the vampire relies upon in order to secure compliant prey. It is critical to remember that once turned, a vampire is no longer human in any traditional sense of the word, and should not be considered constructive to your well-being. This is particularly true should the creature be one that you were familiar with when it was a human, such as a family member, loved one, or friend. As difficult as it may be, you must separate your feelings for the individual you once knew from the creature standing before you.

TRANSFORMATION

Although much is still unknown regarding the transmission that initiates the transformation process from human into vampire, one fact that has been confirmed is that it is morphogenetic in nature. Often used to describe the embryonic development of an organism, morphogenesis can occur in mature creatures as a result of exposure to certain elements, such as hormones, pollutants, or toxic chemicals, like those from a vampire when it releases the transforming agents into the victim's bloodstream. While it may seem almost mystical that this metamorphosis is able to so dramatically alter the Homo sapien form into its vampire state, morphogenetic transformations are a common occurrence throughout nature. The vampire's phenotypic plasticity, its ability to adapt in response to changes in its environment, occurs often in other organisms that must

II. ANATOMY

survive nature's elements. As we dispelled in the section on Misconceptions, the compounds that activate the conversion process are intentionally transmitted by the host organism; should you suffer a bite from an attacking vampire during a combat engagement, you will not automatically become a member of the species. It is also known that the only transmittal mechanism is via perforation of the skin by the subject's maxillary canines, or fangs, and not through other common methods of bacterial transmission such as airborne transference, scratches, or inadvertent contact with vampiric fluids. Once the biological alterations within the human body resulting from the turning process are complete, the creature possesses several traits indicative of this unique species.

Life Span

The conversion process causes a sweeping transmutation in the human body down to the cellular level. This mutative process prepares the corporal structure of the newly turned vampire to feed on its sole source of nourishment. This mutation also enables the individual undead cells to survive for a much longer period of time than the average human cell and repair themselves as required, as long as an adequate level of nutrients is provided. This protracted life span for its various tissues and organs is what enables the vampire to survive for hundreds, if not thousands, of years. While it may seem inconceivable that an organism could exist for such an extended life span, it has been hypothesized that this vampire trait is the counter-reaction to diseases such as Werner's syndrome, Cockayne's syndrome, and other "accelerated aging" diseases that cause the human body to age dramatically in a short period of time. Interestingly, those suffering from these aging diseases also show a strong sensitivity to ultraviolet light.

Digestion

As part of the conversion process, the digestive system mutates from that of an omnivorous being to one that requires only a single source of energy to exist. The organelles within every vampire cell adapt to serve a singular purpose: to process nutrients from this food source with high efficiency. Thus, vampires no longer 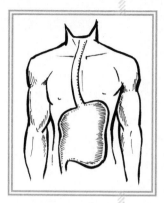 need to digest food or ingest water to survive. The organs that were once responsible for absorbing the complex blend of nutrients required by the human body transform into structures whose primary purpose is to store and process the maximum quantity of blood possible to sustain its undead host. The stomach expands significantly, while the small and large intestines retract, as the absorption tasks they once performed are no longer required, effectively becoming vestigial organs. Interestingly, the human appendix also seems to serve a purpose in vampire digestion, leading some to believe that there lies a deeper, unknown history of the human body in relation to our vampiric counterparts.

Predation

Like many evolutionary processes, the conversion process not only transforms the vampire body's ability to digest its new energy source; it also maximizes the creature's ability to effectively stalk the source of this nourishment. Much the same way a cheetah's hindquarters or a crocodile's tail enables it to hunt its prey efficiently in its native environment, a vampire is provided all the necessary physical assets to pursue, hunt, and bring down its human prey. We will discuss these specific assets in further detail later in this section.

II. ANATOMY

Mental Trauma

While the physiological effects of vampire conversion are static and documented, the psychological effects of conversion are less consistent and largely unknown by the general populace. The majority of vampire converts are still aware of their prior human existence and the connections to that former life, but are victims of their newfound thirst, and exist solely to satiate it. This leads to marked psychological trauma for many members of the undead, leading researchers to believe that most vampires suffer from some level of post-traumatic stress disorder (PTSD). Tragically for the creature, this type of PTSD is almost always left untreated, and suffered for an eternity.

There are also those humans who, once converted, become "renunciates," vampires that fully embrace their transformation despite the sacrifices required and the necessary adjustments that their new lifestyle entails. Most renunciates are those whose human lives were extremely dissatisfying or unsuccessful. Research has also shown that renunciates exhibit traits commonly associated with psychopathic behavior. Dr. Robert Hare, a psychologist focusing on the field of psychopathy, developed a checklist of behaviors exhibited by psychopathic individuals, called the Hare Psychopathic Checklist, Revised (PCL-R). In comparing the PCL-R against renunciate behavior, a high correlation emerges. Some commonalities between undead traits and the checklist behaviors include:

- Callousness; lack of empathy
- Superficial charm
- Cunning/Manipulative
- Lack of remorse/guilt

- Parasitic lifestyle
- Poor behavioral control
- Impulsivity/Irresponsibility
- Grandiose sense of self-worth

STRENGTHS

Once the conversion process is complete, the nascent creature has a set of newly acquired physical assets that enable it to survive within its environment and hunt its victims in order to satisfy its requirement for sustenance. These assets are what make a vampire such an intimidating opponent, and an undead engagement so dangerous to the human species. Take note of these strengths and their impact in combat, as they will be used to the fullest extent by your adversary.

Healing

Of the many physical advantages a vampire possesses, its enhanced healing factor is often the most disconcerting to a human opponent during a combat engagement. Once turned, the creature's physical structure is impervious to nearly all types of damage that would leave an ordinary person completely incapacitated or near death. The vampire's curative factor is extraordinarily rapid, with trivial abrasions healing instantaneously, minor wounds closing within minutes, and more extensive damage completely repaired in a matter of hours. This ability makes a vampire invulnerable to most hand-to-hand and ballistic weaponry, including a majority of firearms.

II. ANATOMY

Fangs

Perhaps the most well-known and universally recognizable attributes of a vampire are the creature's modified upper maxillary canines, otherwise known as its fangs. This physical asset is the primary tool used by the undead to feed upon its prey. Although a vampire's fangs are renowned even among individuals with limited undead knowledge, they

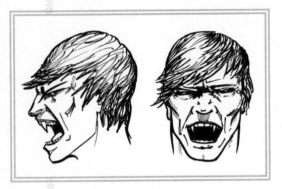

are still often misunderstood in their application. All mammals are equipped with what are known as cuspids, or "eyeteeth" for their position under the eyes. Longer and pointier than the neighboring incisors, their length and shape denote a singular purpose: to firmly retain prey and tear it apart. Although humans have evolved to a point where the cuspids are barely distinguishable from the adjoining teeth, in other species such as tigers, wolves, and bears, the canines continue to serve their much needed purpose in the wild.

While it may appear that a vampire's fangs are an evolution of the creature from its Homo sapien form, it is more accurately stated that upon conversion, the human de-evolves, returning to a more primal state where sharp canines are an essential factor to its hunting ability. Approximately six to eight millimeters longer than standard human canines, the teeth themselves do not extend or retract as commonly depicted in the media, nor are they hollow like the fangs of a poisonous serpent. As with other predatory animals, a vampire's fangs are ever-present, although some members of the species may use dental prosthetics to mask their pronounced length in order to further blend into human society. Their application is similar to the use of the canines by a wild animal: to secure its victim and tear at the flesh in order to cause extensive soft tissue damage, with the goal of opening a major artery. Once a primary bloodline has been accessed, the vampire will draw from the open wound into its throat, not siphoning through the fangs themselves. While there are some rumors that the bacterial compounds that cause human conversion originate from a vampire's fangs, this has not yet been verified through any formal laboratory analysis.

Fingers

During the transformation process, the digits on the human hand undergo a slight change in their structure. Specifically, the middle and ring fin-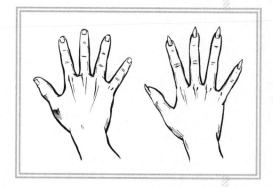gers on a vampire elongate until they are nearly equal in length. While the exact purpose of this physical alteration is unknown, IUCS researchers have determined that the additional length provides assistance in grasping and immobilizing human prey. Witnesses have claimed to have seen a vampire lock a single hand around the throat of a victim and, by compressing the carotid arteries on both sides of the neck between thumb and middle finger, cause its victim to lose consciousness. Additionally, many creatures allow their nails to grow to clawlike lengths, which they further file down to lethal points, providing the vampire an additional set of tools with which to hunt.

II. ANATOMY

Physical Augmentation

The conversion from human into vampire brings about a radical alteration in the physical structure of the subject's body. Still Homo sapiens in superficial form, nearly all of a vampire's physical attributes are enhanced once the morphogenesis is complete. Vision, hearing, strength, and speed are all amplified in the creature, with the average vampire gaining anywhere from two to three times its previous human level of physical prowess. In other words, a human who can bench-press one hundred pounds would be able to press anywhere from two to three hundred pounds as a vampire. It is important to note that these physical enhancements are maximized primarily during nocturnal hours. During daylight, the creature's physical prowess, while still elevated, will not be completely enhanced until the sun has set.

Pain Tolerance

Just as the transformation enhances all the positive physical traits of the vampire, it also diminishes those traits that would have a negative impact on the creature in combat. A significant change is the dramatic reduction in the number of nociceptors, sensory pain receptors, throughout the vampire body. As a result, the creature is able to withstand most superficial traumas to its epidermal layer without so much as a wince of discomfort. It has been rumored that the maximum pain threshold a vampire is able to withstand is nearly three times that of an ordinary human being. Coupled with its superior healing factor, this ability to withstand marked levels of trauma makes the vampire a fearsome opponent in hand-to-hand combat.

Beast Control

As we clarified in the opening chapter on Misconceptions, vampires do not have the ability to mutate into other life-forms. How then did this myth become so mainstream among even casual observers of vampire lore? Although they are unable to turn themselves into other animal forms, what these creatures do seem to possess is an innate ability to communicate with and control certain animal classes.

Wolves, rodents, bats, and other nocturnal creatures are particularly susceptible to their influence. Does this signify some particular extraordinary sensory ability possessed by the vampire? Perhaps. A more logical conclusion is that, through hundreds of years and dedication to practice, vampires have acquired the ability to train other creatures to do their bidding, much like an animal trainer. With hundreds of years to dedicate to refining this ability, it is no wonder that vampires are experts at command-

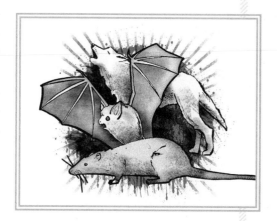

ing these lesser life-forms. It also appears that this skill can extend to control over humans as well. Often the weak-willed and feebleminded are recruited by the species to do the bidding of their controller, executing orders that the vampire is either unwilling or unable to do itself due to its physical limitations.

Should this theory sound illogical, consider again the fact that the vampire has a virtual eternity to hone its field of study, be it psychology, combat, or even operant training of

II. ANATOMY

beasts, such as in the witness statement below taken from an official police record.

4/13/87

4:37 A.M.

Witness Description: Caucasian Male, 28, BAC .07%

Statement of the Witness: Witness claims he and three companions were departing Flaherty's Pub at 3:30 A.M. Screams heard coming from adjoining alleyway. Witnesses saw assailant, male, pinning victim, female, also bar patron, against the wall. Assailant was pulling at victim's hair and ripping open the top of her shirt. Witness party yelled, interrupting assault. Assailant began to flee, with witnesses in pursuit. Assailant ran for half a block, turned into an alley on Thirty-second Street leading to a fenced gate. Assailant turned toward witness in hostile manner. Witness party grabbed objects to defend themselves, including one bottle, a piece of rebar, and broken pieces of lumber. Assailant stepped back into the shadow of the building. Within seconds, rats came from the shadowed area where assailant retreated, toward the witness party. When the rodents were gone, assailant had disappeared. Witness claims, "It was like he disappeared into the shadows." Upon returning to location of assault, victim had also fled the scene.

Human Assistance

While not an intrinsic trait developed via the conversion process, the fact remains that vampires often do have a powerful affiliation with and control over certain humans. These individuals, either completely enamored of the creature's mythological reputation and/or physical attributes, or seeking something in return from the creature, will often perform tasks that the vampire itself cannot easily complete, including any undertaking that requires activity during daylight hours. As a potential target, be aware that these types of individuals exist and behave at the behest of their "master," performing duties that often include securing prospective targets during daylight hours. Simply because the sun is high does not necessarily mean that you are insulated from a vampire's clutches.

COMBAT REPORT: NATHAN FIRESTONE

Private Military Contractor
Baghdad, Iraq

I sit outside a teahouse bordering the area once known as the International, or "Green," zone in Eastern Iraq. The heat is near incapacitating. As I wipe the sweat off my brow with my shemagh, I look up at the exterior façade of the café. Its appearance does not provide a strong sense of security for the outdoor patrons. The shop's awning flutters in tatters. The walls are heavily pockmarked from artillery and mortar fire, with immense chunks missing from the walls. This damage, however, does not cause as much anxiety as the intense glaring from the other patrons, who note my conspicuous presence. Despite having received detailed instruction on local customs and proper attire so as not to draw unwarranted attention, it is clear that I am not very convincing. Their gazes are interrupted only by the harsh blast of a sandstorm, which seems to erupt out of nowhere, causing the patrons to cover their teacups and shield their eyes from the biting shower of dust. The storm dissipates as quickly as it came, and the glaring resumes.

Despite the intense heat, blinding storms, and the risk of violence from open exposure to the street, I was told not to venture inside the café under any circumstances. Such were the specific instructions of my contact, Nathan Firestone, a PMC, or private military contractor. As the minutes tick by, I grow increasingly concerned that Firestone has changed his mind about our meet. My anxiety intensifies as I observe that the individuals who took note of my presence are now speaking on their mobile phones, all the while staring at me unflinchingly. I am seconds from taking my leave when I feel a hand on my shoulder, pressing me back into my seat.

Unlike myself, Firestone is indistinguishable from the indigenous population. I realize in the few moments observing him that he has not only the attire but also the cultural mannerisms of a local that come only from years of operating in the region. As with many PMCs, his past includes decades of experience in military special operations, battling through war-torn regions across the globe, including our current location. He sits and beckons the proprietor, ordering in fluent Arabic. The locals who previously took such interest in my presence seem to be less concerned now that Firestone has arrived.

Nathan Firestone: It's amazing what people will believe. Tell them the world's most wanted man evaded the world's most powerful military, they believe it. Tell them he's been living in a mountain cave with a faltering kidney for ten years, they believe it. Tell them he was killed in a raid in Pakistan. . . .

The shop owner arrives with Firestone's order. A cup of Iraqi tea is set in front of me. What appears to be a glass filled only with hot water is placed in front of Firestone. He reaches into his dishdasha shirt and removes a gleaming dagger. The silver blade reflects the sun's rays brightly. He retrieves a head of garlic from his pocket, snaps off two cloves, and begins slicing them thinly with the knife, allowing the slivers to drop into his glass.

NF: I had just finished up a six-month personal security contract in Germany. As much as I like drawing a paycheck by looking rough and standing in front of some pop star, my finger was getting the itch again. That's when I got the call from my handler. Black operation, snatch and grab, exactly the type of op I was hoping to find. Be careful what you wish for, as they say. Do you remember how long they reported it took to complete the raid?

Vampire Combat Manual: I believe it was about an hour.

NF: Forty minutes. Probably the only accurate fact that was released, and not a single person questioned it. Forty minutes to breach a three-story compound, sweep an unconfirmed layout, and bag the target. Even with SATINT, thermal imaging, and a platoon of Tier-1 operators, there's no way in hell an operation that complex could be completed in that time frame. Not without months of planning, detailed blueprints, and a full mockup of the target compound, none of which we had, despite what you heard on the news. Not to mention the fact that we had no idea if there was a tunnel network underneath the compound itself, or if any rooms were laced with booby traps or IEDs. Hell, they even admitted that they were only fifty percent certain that the target was present. Even an armchair operator could tell you that there was no way this operation could have been completed successfully without deep familiarity of the compound and the presence of the target. That's where our

II. ANATOMY

ace in the hole comes in. The courier.

I arrived on-site expecting a full briefing, mission rehearsal, and weeks to prepare for the assault. I was told we were going to be wheels up in twenty-four hours. It was ridiculous, bordering on suicidal. Two other contractors and myself were also playing a very specific role in the operation: escort the courier. He would be our primary to direct us through the compound and lead us to the target.

VCM: Why were you selected?

Firestone narrows his gaze, clearly irritated by the question.

VCM: What I mean is, why the need for contractors in a military operation?
NF: The same reason why we're always needed. Sure, DEVGRU[1] was there, as was Delta and the Agency, but it was pretty clear that contractors were going to be working the ugliest part of the op. You may think our participation is used solely for plausible deniability just in case things go sideways, but that isn't the case. If you're an operator on a mission like this, you already know that if you're KIA, the world won't know a damn thing about it. At best, your family will learn that you were killed on a "training mission." The reason contractors like us are used is a much simpler one: money. It costs the government more than a million dollars to train your standard special operations soldier, never mind the top-tier operators. Uncle Sam doesn't like to risk his investment unnecessarily. Once operators go private sector, though, we're a line item on someone else's balance sheet.

Thirty minutes before mission launch, the other contractors and I rendezvous with the courier at a location two klicks from the compound. He looks no different than any other

---

1 DEVGRU: United States Naval Special Warfare Development Group, commonly known as SEAL Team Six.

Pakistani male dressed in customary attire: a dark, loose tunic and baggy trousers. His face is obscured by a keffiyeh head scarf, he's carrying no visible weapons, and he's wearing sandals on his feet. I nearly burst out laughing. This guy, who looks like he'd get winded carrying a ten-pound ruck, is team leader on this operation?

Firestone takes a sip of his garlic-steeped water. His lips come away from the glass with a slice of the clove between his teeth, which he promptly chews and swallows.

NF: We make our way to the target and wait for the signal to breach the compound. The plan is simple—while two teams of operators fast-rope into the front of the compound and launch a forward assault to draw firepower away from the building, the courier would guide the PMC team through a rear entrance and lead us to our target. As we waited for the helos to take position, the courier reached into his pocket and showed me a pack of infrared Glint tape. He speaks the only words he'll say to me during the entire operation: "Follow the marker." I'm about to ask him what he's talking about when we hear the Blackhawks overhead.

Firestone takes a long pause, seeming to reflect on what he's revealing, and perhaps deciding if he wants to share these memories further. He continues.

NF: I've been in this business a long time; worked alongside some of the best operators on the planet. Men who could thread needles with their shots and put Olympic decathletes to shame. I have never seen anyone like the courier. It wasn't only his speed, but the way his body moved, almost animalistic in nature. The minute we were inside the exterior walls of the complex, we were struggling to keep up with him. The courier made his way to a fuse box and cut the power to the compound, literally ripping the power line off the wall. We followed him to a rear entrance into one building when we began to take fire from sentries inside. That's when he disappears. The other two contractors were hit, so I'm the only one left to advance. I turn on my NVGs and hear the courier's voice in my head. "Follow the marker."

Firestone casually unsheathes his knife from his pocket again and turns it in his hands.

NF: I followed the bright glow of the IR tape left by the courier, leading me on a complex maze through three expansive floors of the compound. As I follow the tape, I realize that without the courier's knowledge of the building's layout, there was no way we could have succeeded. Along the way, bodies of sentries lie neutralized. Some have their heads completely twisted in the opposite direction; others are bleeding out from vicious throat wounds, as if they were clawed open. Three different times along the route, I encounter trip wires that have been already tagged and defused by the courier. I arrive at a doorway where the bodies of several guards lie at the entrance. A scream comes from inside the room. I draw my P226 and enter to a sight that is forever burned into my memory.

The courier's back is toward me when I enter the room. In front of him is our target, wrapped in the courier's arms. His arms are splayed out, almost in a pleading gesture. His chin rests on the courier's shoulder. There is a look of terror in his eyes. He sees me and utters in Arabic, *"Saa'adini."* I pull the courier off our target, causing a stream of blood to spray across my eyes, blinding me for a moment. The courier takes the opportunity to grab my Sig and fires two rounds into the chest of the target. I step back and raise my M4 toward the courier, who places my sidearm slowly on the ground and raises his arms. I pause, trying to process what just happened, and figure out what the hell I should do next. I decide to proceed with the biometric scan, which confirms the identity of our target. I tell the courier that I'm still going to need DNA verification, and he removes a set of heavy wire cutters from his sleeve pocket. He casually snaps off the index finger of the target's right hand and stuffs it into one of my vest's magazine pockets.

Additional guards arrive at the doorway. They see their boss on the ground and are none too happy about it. They immediately begin spraying the room with AK fire. I'm hit in the shoulder, but manage to find cover behind a large desk, while the courier retrieves my Sig and fires back at the men, causing them to retreat back into the hallway. Before they have an opportunity to reload and open fire again, the courier picks me up around my rib cage, and leaps backward out of the window. We fall three stories onto the compacted dirt, my fall broken by the courier's own body. He fireman-carries me over his shoulders and retrieves the other two wounded contractors, pulling all three of us to the extraction point. He saved all our lives that night.

Three hours later, I'm standing with my arm in a sling alongside the courier and two of his "associates" in Bahali, a tiny village buried in a valley between the Pakistani mountains. Idling along the dusty road, a tanker truck arrives, followed closely by an MRAP vehicle. The tanker driver, clearly an Agency man, steps out of the cab. He walks to the MRAP and retrieves two large black duffel bags, which he tosses at the feet of the courier. One of the associates scrambles up to the top of the tanker, opens the top of the rig, and dips his arm into the tank, inspecting its contents. In the low light of the moon, I see him withdraw his arm. It is covered in a viscous fluid, which appears black in the moonlit sky. The associate removes his scarf from around his mouth and touches his finger lightly to his tongue. He nods his approval to the courier, who picks up the two duffel bags. The three of them enter the tanker's cab, the contract complete. The courier looks back into my direction once and locks eyes with me, and then drives off. I climb into the MRAP with the Agency man and head back to base. Neither of us says a word during the two-hour drive.

VCM: It would appear your mission was a success.
NF: Would it, now?

Firestone reaches into a cloth sack and places three photographs on the table. They appear to be taken from satellite imagery.

NF: A friend of mine from the NGA[2] gave these to me. They were taken about a week ago in Afghanistan about a mile from the Khyber Pass.

I peer closely at one of the images, which appears to be a group of men at night, riding on horseback. One of the figures in the group looks taller than the rest. I pick up one of the other images, which appears to be a close-up of the tall figure's right hand holding the reins of the saddle. The index finger is missing.

NF: I'm not an idealist. I know how the world works. To catch a demon, sometimes you have to make deals with the devil. As long as my checks clear, I'm not one for asking questions no one wants answered. But there's something else going on, something a hell of a lot bigger, and I'm not the only one beginning to notice. I'm talking to you because, when all is said and done, we may not be the ones calling the shots anymore.

VCM: "We" being the United States?
NF: "We" being the human race.

Another, larger sandstorm begins to swirl in the distance, causing the other patrons to retreat inside the café. The proprietor closes the entrance doors and shutters the windows. Firestone and I find

---

2 NGA: National Geospatial-Intelligence Agency

ourselves alone in front of the shop. I motion for us to retreat with the others into the teahouse, but he does not move. Fierce winds begin to howl around us as we both shield our faces from the stinging granules whipping through the air.

Suddenly, as if formed from the whirling dervishes of sand, a tan Suburban materializes from the dust. Its windows are tinted black, except for the one closest to us, out of which the barrels of several automatic machine guns appear. They open fire.

I instinctively flatten my body against the ground and lay the side of my head against the dirt. I anticipate the snap of bullets as they break the sound barrier passing close by my ear. Seconds later, the vehicle is gone, along with the storm that camouflaged it. As I stand and perform a quick body check for wounds, I notice that Firestone is nowhere to be found. From the corner of my eye, I notice a smear of blood on the teahouse wall. I follow the mark, which turns into a blood trail. The trail eventually leads me to what Firestone seems to have wanted me to find. The blade he was using for his garlic tea is embedded into a wooden garbage crate. I extract the knife, place it into my satchel and depart. Not bothering to return to my hotel, I head straight for Baghdad International Airport with the feeling that I, like Firestone, may have overstayed my welcome.

WEAKNESSES

Having reviewed the strengths possessed by your undead adversary, you may be experiencing a sense of despair at the prospect of engaging in combat with this species. How is it possible for the average human to triumph against a creature with such considerable physical advantages? While the strengths of your opponent are indeed powerful and may seem insurmountable in combat, its weaknesses are equally striking. With the proper intelligence, strategy, and execution of technique, the ordinary citizen has a superb chance to end a combat engagement in his favor, provided he exploits the ghoul's liabilities to their maximum.

It is also crucial to remember that your opponent is not oblivious to its own peril. The reason vampires have been able to exist for centuries is that they have a keen understanding of their own weaknesses and attempt to minimize them at all times. Regardless, armed with the following details on your adversary's flaws, you can enter a vampire engagement with the confidence to emerge victorious and alive.

Ultraviolet Light

Of all the creature's weaknesses, a vampire's incapacity to withstand exposure to ultraviolet (UV) light is the most noteworthy. All members of the vampire species suffer from an extreme form of *xeroderma pigmentosum*—the inability to repair cellular damage caused by exposure to UV radiation. Any protracted exposure to UV light will set off a chemical reaction that causes the creature's exposed epidermal layer to oxidize and combust within a matter of seconds. Based on recorded empirical data, the following timing sequence occurs during a vampire's exposure to UV light:

- **1–10 seconds:** third-degree burns
- **10–20 seconds:** spontaneous combustion
- **30+ seconds:** complete immolation

While the specific activators that cause this violent reaction have yet to be analyzed, it is apparent that UV light has a powerful effect on the undead species. It is surmised that the reaction is similar to the use of light to eliminate bacteria and as a disinfecting germicidal agent—albeit in a much more powerful context. Whatever the reason for this reaction, this liability not only enables a human combatant to leverage a powerful ally in the warming rays of the Earth's sun; it also keeps the undead at bay for roughly half the operating day, allowing humans to go about business in broad daylight with little concern of being attacked by a voracious ghoul.

However, it is not only direct exposure to the sun's ultraviolet rays that makes the daylight hours a liability for the undead. A vampire's biorhythm, its physical clock cycle, seems to be directly tied to the rising and setting of earth's heat source. Thus, a vampire's physical advantages seem to ebb and flow as the hours pass from sunset until sunrise. It comes as no surprise, then, that most

vampire attacks occur between the hours of midnight and three A.M., when the creature's physical biorhythm is at its peak. Conversely, a vampire will grow increasingly vulnerable closer to the hours of sunrise as its physical cycle begins to wane. The creature is at its weakest when the sun's ultraviolet rays are at their peak, approximately twelve P.M. to three P.M. Understanding the creature's physical cycles can help you ascertain your level of vulnerability during a combat entanglement with the undead.

While the rays of the sun are the most obvious source of UV light, they are not the only source. Due to the growing popularity of indoor gardening, many artificial sources of ultraviolet light are now available to the public in the forms of fabricated lamps, beams, and light bulbs. These sources can be just as effective as the light of the sun, if not more so due to their portability. Be cautious in their use, as exposure to UV light through these portable devices can be as damaging to a human's skin and eyes as the rays of the sun. They are also notoriously fragile; wielding such a device in the heat of vampire combat will in most cases cause your opponent to shatter the light source before mounting its counterattack.

Garlic

A member of the onion family, *Allium sativum* has been prized for centuries not only as a culinary ingredient, but also as a natural healing agent. Although its dietary uses

are evident and commonplace, this unique plant also has a storied reputation dating back to the Egyptians for its antibacterial and antiviral properties, and was used as an antiseptic agent during both the first and second world wars. There have been many studies conducted on the general medicinal benefits of the plant aside from its use against the undead. Garlic has been claimed to be an effective preventative agent for many ailments, including high cholesterol, cancer, heart disease, and hypertension, which may be related to the repulsion felt by the creature toward this healing plant. All vampires by nature suffer from a condition known as "alliumphobia," fear of garlic. While this phobia is commonly thought of as irrational in humans, it is most certainly understandable for this particular species. Creatures that come into direct contact with the plant, particularly the fresh, peeled cloves, seem to experience an intense burning or caustic reaction, the approximate equivalent being a human exposed to a severe chemical agent such as phenacyl chloride, otherwise known as CN gas.

Based on the strong objectionable reaction to the plant by your undead adversary, allium sativum can be a powerful weapon in your arsenal, provided it is utilized properly. Peeled, raw cloves from the fresh bulb are abhorrent to your opponent. Even more effective are cloves that have been finely chopped or diced, releasing the chemical properties of the plant. Garlic powder, cooked garlic, or garlic pills are poor substitutes for the fresh item.

Silver

Silver has been coveted throughout history for both its decorative and antimicrobial properties. The ancient Phoenicians were said to have stored wine in silver-lined containers to prevent spoilage. Similar to garlic, the silver element was also used as an infection preventive during World War I before the advent of antibiotics. In your battle with the undead, silver can be as intimidating to the vampire as it is alluring to humans.

II. ANATOMY

Research has not identified the exact property that causes such a corrosive reaction in vampires, but it is believed that silver causes an accelerated oligodynamic effect—literally having a toxic reaction on the undead cellular structure. This same result can be seen in humans exposed to extensive quantities of lead or mercury. The effect on vampires, however, is much more immediate and dynamic.

Although powerful, the ability of silver to neutralize a vampire must be qualified. Silver causes an acerbic reaction on wounds inflicted on a vampire. Blows that would heal straightaway with an ordinary weapon will remain open when silver is incorporated. The result is similar to cauterization by fire or a chemical burn, destroying the epidermal layer and surrounding cell walls. However, it is critical to note that silver does *not* have the same neutralizing effect on the undead when attacking the creature's most vulnerable organ: its heart. This is an important distinction that we will explore later in further detail.

Bloodlust

While it is fairly common knowledge that a vampire requires human blood to subsist, the exact feeding frequency has never been fully examined, due to the limited number of test subjects willing to divulge such information. Based on empirical data derived from recorded attacks, IUCS researchers have determined that the average vampire consuming four pints of blood from its victim can go without replenishment for a maximum of seventy-two hours. Should the creature consume more than this quantity in a single feeding session, the period before the next required feeding is extended. As the average human body contains approximately eight to twelve pints of blood, a vampire could go without feeding for approximately six to nine days should it drain its victim entirely.

What often occurs, however, is that a vampire's feeding is interrupted, causing it to halt its meal before it is satiated. Should a vampire not be able to nourish its body in the requisite number of hours, a painful condition known as *strigis anaemia* sets in, known in layman's terms as "bloodlust." This condition causes the creature's body to begin cannibalizing itself, weakening its ability to hunt. In a self-perpetuating cycle, the weakened vampire can no longer hunt effectively, and as a result cannot adequately nourish itself. A creature that has gone an average of three days past its required replenishment point will consume itself entirely. While there is no human equivalent to the physical symptoms a vampire experiences from strigis anaemia, the closest human approximation is the suffering associated with severe dehydration, although it is rumored that this human condition still pales in comparison to the agony experienced by a vampire unable to quench its thirst.

A vampire is forever tethered to its insatiable need to feed, a trait that intelligent warriors can leverage in undead combat.

Physical Stasis

We have spent a considerable amount of time emphasizing the unique physical abilities of your opponent. This emphasis is not meant to discourage or dishearten you, but to ensure you fully grasp the fact that these attributes cannot be determined from outward appearances alone. In fact, many humans fall victim to their undead attacker in a combat engagement as a result of underestimating its strength, speed, and stamina.

Despite its superior physicality, there is a weakness exhibited by the creature's anatomy once it has converted from human being to vampire. As discussed earlier, the physical characteristics of a succubus seem to increase by a factor of

II. ANATOMY

two or three from its previous human form. However, once full conversion has taken place, a vampire cannot continue to improve its physical abilities through strength training and conditioning routines; in other words, a vampire's strength will remain static for the remainder of its existence. An undead creature that can bench-press 200 pounds will forever be able to press only 200 pounds. On the other hand, human beings can continue to improve upon their physical abilities as much as their bodies and time allow.

BEHAVIORAL TRAITS

In addition to the corporal alterations undergone by humans turned into the undead, there are a number of psychological qualities that are consistently exhibited by the vampire species regardless of historical setting or geographic origin. Just as it is critical to understand the physical traits of your adversary in order to successfully engage it in combat, being mindful of these behaviors can provide a deeper insight into the attack strategies of your opponent, as well as enable you to leverage these traits to develop a successful counterattack.

Homesteading

A vampire is at its greatest vulnerability in the immediate moments after the conversion process is complete. At this stage, the creature's cellular structure is no longer human, but its internal vampiric structure has not yet begun taking in nutrients from its preferred food source. Couple this with a metamorphosis that is incredibly debilitating to the creature's physiology, and you have a being that requires immediate nourishment or risks physical collapse, much like a newborn animal. It is for this reason that as part of the conversion process, vampires practice a behavior known as "homesteading."

As you will learn later in this text, a vampire is unable to physically enter a human's residence without an expressed invitation from a member of the household. When a vampire homesteads, it will seek out the residence of its loved ones, relying on the probability that the creature will be known to the individuals residing at that location, and welcome it with open arms. Once inside, the vampire will commence its inaugural feeding. Prior to the research conducted into the practice of homesteading, it was believed that the vampire returned home in order to search for individuals from its human existence, perhaps looking for comfort or assistance. We now know that a vampire's return home is solely an innate survival tactic built into the conversion process so that the creature is able to locate a likely source of nourishment that will enable it to survive its rebirth as a member of the undead.

It is vital that should you encounter any unusual behavior on the part of a roommate, friend, or loved one (i.e., arriving at the doorstep in the late evening hours, asking for permission to enter the residence), consider the possibility that he or she may be a recently converted succubus seeking the first meal of its new existence.

Arrogance

As self-aware, albeit undead, beings, vampires are well familiar with the superior attributes they possess over their human counterparts. This usually leads members of the species to develop an air of preeminence, exemplified by a casual and unthreatened attitude when confronted by human adversaries looking to terminate their existence. The sad truth is that often a vampire's egoism is supported by its successes in combat.

This conceit, however, can also serve as a severe liability. The primary reason the undead feel little to no threat from the human race is that the majority of our society is either unaware of or unschooled in the tactics of undead combat. As a result, vampires often place themselves in vulnerable positions, believing that their victims are too dim-witted or inexperienced to capitalize on the situation. Those of you who study and apply the material contained within these pages represent the minority of individuals educated in the art of vampire combat, and can use your adversary's overconfidence to your advantage.

Bloodrage

Just as its physical attributes may cause the undead to possess an arrogance when it comes to the threat posed by humanity, these attributes can also cause it to be reckless during combat. The creature's belief that any human opponent regardless of skill is easily defeated causes a vampire to often attack haphazardly during a hostile engagement. Rather than

utilize any form of technique, vampires rely on their physical prowess to overwhelm their victims. This wanton behavior is more prevalent in vampires who have not fed in a timely manner; the lack of nourishment impairs their combat skills and the desperate need to feed clouds their ability to attack strategically. While an unruly, undisciplined attack may be intimidating to the inexperienced opponent, a trained vampire combatant can exploit this behavior to expose gaps in his undead foe. The key to taking advantage of this weakness is to remain calm in the heat of battle, and trust that your disciplined approach will overcome any physical superiority your opponent may have during its frenzied attack.

A hungry vampire is also a desperate vampire. The longer the desperation continues, the more enraged your opponent will become. Should a vampire go without feeding for the requisite amount of time, a condition researchers have termed "bloodrage" begins to emerge. Predatory instincts ignite within the creature, enhancing all its hunting capabilities to maximize its ability to secure an imminent kill.

The condition can be easily recognized in an undead opponent by its erratic and violent movements and the uncontrolled gnashing of its jaws. At this moment, there is no question that your adversary is at its most lethal. Unfortunately, your ability to recognize this condition in your opponent also means that you are in close enough proximity to be its next victim.

Nevertheless, do not despair. In most instances, a vampire exhibits bloodrage because it has not properly fed and as a result, its body has initiated the cannibalization process, leaving the creature weaker than when at peak condition. While bloodrage could be considered a strength of the vampire, the strategic combatant can also use this condition to his or her advantage, leveraging the creature's recklessness to lure it into an unfavorable position. An untrained civilian witnessing a bloodraging vampire sees violence and mayhem; the trained vampire combatant witnessing the same sees an opportunity to end the threat.

II. ANATOMY

VULNERABILITIES

Having detailed your opponent's general strengths and liabilities, we can now delve into the vulnerabilities and target areas that will influence your overall combat strategy. The mutation process that is responsible for transforming the creature is an extraordinarily intelligent one; it provides your opponent with a wealth of offensive assets while minimizing its liabilities. There are woefully few areas you can attack that can swiftly eliminate your opponent. The only methods to end a hand-to-hand combat encounter with a vampire are to pierce its heart with a wood-based weapon, separate its head from its torso, or expose it to UV light. Let us delve into each of these vulnerabilities in further detail, as well as explore other factors that can limit a vampire's ability to feed.

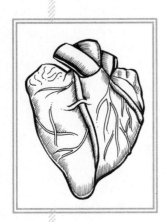

The Vampire Heart

There is no question that in a close-combat vampire encounter, your primary attack target should be the creature's heart. In the human species, this organ is responsible for managing the circulatory system, delivering nutrients and oxygenated blood throughout the body. While the vampire heart still retains some accountability for this circulatory task, it does not function as it did prior to the subject's transformation. Since a vampire does not require oxygen to survive, its heart serves a different purpose. Although detailed research is still pending, it seems that this organ operates in coordination with the creature's mutated digestive system to deliver nutrients and energy ingested from its feedings to the rest of its undead body.

One of the most well-known legends of vampire lore is that driving a sharpened object into the undead heart will end the creature's existence. Although many elements of vampire fables are complete fabrications, in this case the myth is indeed accurate. It is unknown why the species has allowed knowledge of what is probably its most critical vulnerability to spread unabated throughout the human population, but it is true that destroying the vampire heart will neutralize your attacker immediately. There is still some confusion surrounding the details of this maneuver, the greatest of which is: What type of sharpened object?

Given the creature's aversion to silver, it is often assumed that a pointed stave crafted from this rare element is effective at eliminating the undead. This is wholly incorrect. While silver and silver-based implements can play a role in your arsenal against the undead, it *will not* neutralize your target. Penetrating the vampire heart with a silver implement, while causing the wound to remain open and decelerating the creature's advanced healing capabilities, will not end the confrontation. This common misconception has caused many brave yet ignorant warriors to fall at the hands of their adversaries just when they believed victory was at hand.

In order to take full advantage of this specific vulnerability, a sharpened object crafted from wood or wood-based material is required. While a detailed chemical analysis regarding the precise compounds contained within the material is still forthcoming, the hypothesis is that the natural resins contained within the fibers of the wood react with the altered chemistry of the vampire's heart, setting off an irrepressible chain reaction resulting in the creature's demise.

II. ANATOMY

Decapitation

The other physical undead vulnerability on which to focus your attack is the head and neck region. When its spinal column is severed and its cranium is completely separated from its torso, a vampire ceases to pose a mortal threat. Once separation is complete, both segments should be permanently destroyed by fire, ultraviolet light, explosives, or mechanical compression. Keep in mind, however, that the actual act of severing a head from its body is more difficult than widely understood, especially on an opponent who is clearly aware of how susceptible this region is, and is actively defending against such an attack.

A combination of factors must be addressed in order to execute a successful decapitation attack, including weapon selection, attacker vulnerability, and skill level of the combatants. Additionally, the time required to deliver a decapitation strike is on average longer than executing a staking blow to the heart. In the later chapters on combat strategy, we will discuss scenarios in which to employ each type of these finishing blows to your bloodthirsty assailant.

Ultraviolet (UV) Light Exposure

As we discussed earlier, a key weakness of the vampire is its inability to handle epidermal exposure to ultraviolet light, particularly light generated by the rays of the Earth's sun. Managing the daylight hours to your advantage and utilizing the sun as your ally can play a significant role in helping you survive a vampire attack. There are also synthetic sources of ultraviolet light available in the form of lamps, flashlights, and head torches that you can employ when mounting your attack.

The time required to completely neutralize your attacker via the use of UV rays depends entirely on the degree and intensity of the light being utilized. Synthetic UV light created from manufactured sources seems to require more exposure time than does pure sunlight, but this may also have to do with the creature's ability to evade prolonged exposure to such sources. UV rays generated by the sun at daybreak also seem to take longer to fully immolate an exposed vampire than when the sun is at its highest peak during the midday hours. Combatants should not be overly concerned during days when the sun is hidden behind heavy cloud cover. Despite a lack of direct sunlight, ultraviolet rays are still penetrating through to the earth's atmosphere with enough intensity to destroy any vampire ignorant enough to expose itself during daylight hours.

Dismemberment

Due to a vampire's accelerated cellular regenerative abilities, minor wounds, cuts, and lacerations suffered by the creature will heal almost instantaneously. However, should an appendage become completely separated from your attacker's torso, the creature does not have the ability to regenerate the lost limb like other life-forms such as Urodela (salamanders) or Echinoderms (starfish). While dismembering a vampire will not neutralize your opponent completely, removing a limb— be it a leg, arm, or hand—will very likely cause your opponent to retreat from its attack, saving you from contending with a protracted combat engagement.

There is an important point to consider when initiating any type of dismembering blow during your engagement. It is quite possible that, given enough time, a limb that is only partially dismembered will repair itself completely. Should you succeed in separating a limb from your adversary, the vampire can in fact reattach the severed appendage to the wound's location if it is able to hold it in place for an

II. ANATOMY

appropriate length of time. Be sure to distance your opponent from its amputated limb to ensure permanent removal. Similar to decapitation, dismembering an attacking vampire also requires that you possess the necessary level of combative skill and appropriate armament to accomplish such a feat.

The Invitation

A curious and unexplained trait of vampire behavior is what researchers have termed domicile histodiscordant reaction (DHR), otherwise known as "the invitation." The layman explanation of this unusual trait is that a vampire standing outside the entrance of a human's residence is unable to enter the premises unless formally invited by a member of said residence. Should the creature attempt to enter without this proper summons, a violent response occurs in the vampire, causing seizures, hematomas, and eventual self-combustion within minutes of crossing the entrance's threshold.

The misconception surrounding this condition is that only the "head of the household" can provide safe passage inside by invitation. In fact, any member of the family that resides at the domicile can literally open the door to the undead. It is precisely this fact that many vampires use to their advantage by convincing younger, more naïve residents, such as children and teenagers, to grant them access, resulting in disastrous consequences.

Researchers theorize that the root cause of this unusual reaction in the undead relates to pheromones continuously released by humans and the corresponding reaction generated in a vampire's vomeronasal organ used to detect said pheromones. During the transformative process, this organ seems to undergo an evolution much like other organs in the creature's physiology. The resulting effect is that in an uninvited home, a vampire experiences an extreme and violent case of anaphylactic shock, causing the creature's nervous system to initiate a complete bleed out and shutdown sequence. While the causes remain unclear, the benefit to humans is quite substantial. What this means to every potential victim is that the safest refuge against a hostile vampiric attacker is one's own home. It is very fortunate that scientists in the creatures' employ have not found an effective countermeasure for DHR, as it is likely that this limitation is the only barrier preventing skyrocketing rates of home invasions by ravenous undead creatures on the hunt. For now, it can be assumed that a vampire is unable to enter your domestic residence unless formally invited, allowing you a safe retreat. Note that this restriction applies only to your personal living quarters, not any random abode, hotel room, or cabin where you may be temporarily residing.

VAMPIRE CASTES

As a result of unmeasured replication and rampant migration in pursuit of available prey, subtle variations of the vampire exist on each of the world's continents. Based on detailed analysis, however, researchers have been able to determine that the species divides itself into five distinct undead castes.

Banals

Of all the different undead segments, the most common by far is the vampire caste known as Banals. Seventy percent of the species encountered fall within this class, which is recognized

by its interchangeability with the normal human form. Banals walk as humans walk, dress as humans dress, and, when night falls, act as humans act, which is exactly what makes them so lethal.

Banals can easily blend into normal society once the sun has set and, besides a slightly opaque pallor, cannot be readily identified in open territory. Many Banals often choose to dress unobtrusively, so as not to draw undesired attention. Appearing as a normal, everyday human can also assist the Banal vampire during its attack, because it can easily approach its victim without causing undue alarm. It is precisely for this reason that the Banal is a difficult opponent to battle. Often underestimated due to the creature's superficial appearance, it has been said that during a Banal vampire attack, the victim usually has no idea what is coming until it is too late.

Another theory regarding the high prevalence of the Banal population is that many vampires within this sect seek to retain some element of their formerly human existence by continuing to dress and act in a manner indicative of their previous life. While this theory is unconfirmed, interviews conducted by the author suggest that this concept may have some merit. *(See Combat Report: Jason Richter.)*

Despite their seemingly unthreatening facade, it is recommended that you not engage any member of this population in deliberate discourse or unwarranted combat. When it comes to the Banal vampire, appearances are absolutely deceiving.

Seducers

Representing only 10 percent of the species, the Seducer comprises a small part of the vampire population. It is, however, the type most frequently depicted by human media. Characterized by their stunningly attractive features and substantial charisma, Seducer vampires are what most humans imagine when asked to picture such a creature—one that is beautiful, charming, and appealing to the last. It is precisely these qualities that Seducers use not only to target their victims,

but to reinforce the idea among the human population that the vampiric lifestyle is an alluring existence. It is no accident that the image of the vampire portrayed on film and television continues to be that of a beautiful, devilish imp, rather than a bloodthirsty, insatiable ghoul.

An important trait of this class that warrants mentioning is the fact that, while Seducers will feed on any type of human available, members of this sect will convert only those humans who qualify appearance-wise to fall into their caste. While

II. ANATOMY

other vampire classes may turn their victims for a variety of reasons, the Seducer is interested only in propagating its own unique sect. All other victims that do not meet the physical qualifications will remain blood fodder, regardless of what the Seducer tells its victim prior to feeding.

Another distinguishing characteristic of the Seducer is the caste's lack of combat experience compared to that of its vampiric counterparts. Their target selection is purposeful, and they mostly utilize charm and guile rather than force and aggression. Victims often hand their bodies over willingly with no resistance, either in the heat of the perceived sexually-charged moment, or with the intention of being converted. Consequently, the Seducer rarely, if ever, needs to assault its victims in order to feed.

It has often been asked if the Seducer class of vampires is capable of having sexual intercourse with their victims. While this concept has also been heavily promoted through the media, it represents yet another ploy by this manipulative adversary, playing to the general public's attraction to the vampire as a sensual, accepting life mate. Although we firmly established this as a misconception in the opening chapter, it bears repeating, particularly when speaking of the Seducer sect: Vampires have no more interest in humans as life partners than humans do in building a life with our food.

Grotesques

A unique subset of the Banal class, creatures in the Grotesque caste represent roughly 15 percent of the vampire population. As their name conveys, ghouls in this sect have some element of disfigurement to their appearance. Due to their deformations, they are often considered pariahs within the vampire community, and are particularly loathed by the Seducer caste. The cause of these deformities is directly related to the quality of the blood ingested by a vampire, and how it is processed through its altered digestive system. The ideal sustenance for a vampire is always fresh human blood. Should a vampire deviate from this high-quality nourishment and ingest the blood of creatures lower on the food chain, the creature's vital systems can be sustained, but distortion of the features about the face and body will result. The more prolonged the feeding on lesser animals, the more extensive the deformations. Even if human blood is reintroduced into the vampire's system, the existing deformations are irreversible.

Why a vampire would choose to feed on any source of blood other than a human is a question that continues to be debated. Most believe that it is simply due to availability of the food supply or the poor hunting skills of that particular creature. Another theory suggests that it may be a more conscious decision made by certain vampires to not feed on humans, despite being fully aware that the result will be the deforming of their own features and becoming outcasts amongst their own kind. This calls into question certain concepts of the undead mentality, and whether a vampire has truly lost all of its human emotional ties once turned. These are difficult questions to answer, and until more comprehensive analyses can be conducted, it must be assumed that humans continue to be vulnerable targets to all vampires, regardless of caste.

II. ANATOMY

Supremists

Representing only 5 percent of the population, Supremists are not only one of the smallest, but are also the most lethal of all vampire castes. The most hostile sect of all the vampire populace, Supremists have not only completely embraced their newfound anatomy, but work their entire immortal existence to refine and develop their strengths in order to achieve their one and only goal: domination of the human race.

Whereas most other castes choose to exist in tandem with the human population, Supremists believe that they represent an evolution of the human species, and work toward growing their numbers in anticipation of the day when they will rule the planet, rather than live in the shadow of it. They spend much of their non-feeding hours developing their physical prowess through training in specific vampire martial arts unavailable to other undead sects and honing their mental acumen with rigorous academic study. It is not uncommon for members of this class to attain advanced educational degrees and doctorates in a wide variety of fields.

Like the Seducer class, Supremists are exceedingly

discriminating when it comes to conversion, and will turn only those who they believe will embrace their caste once a member and contribute something of significance to their cause, whether it be their physical skills or mental intellect. Those who do not meet their standards are promptly neutralized. While sightings of this class are rare, the Supremist is said to be larger and more imposing than most vampires, an example of the selective process by which members are turned. It has been said that this class, though few in number, is the most skilled and educated of the undead population—a powerful statement considering the immortal nature of the creature itself. Rumor has it that Supremists are simply biding their time until the ideal moment to execute their master plan. Whatever the details of such a plan may be, the intended outcome does not bode well for their source of nourishment.

Elders

The least known and most mysterious of the vampire classes, Elders are near mythic in their existence, even among the vampire community itself. It has been said that creatures in this class have existed for thousands of years, some dating back to biblical ages. Their protracted survival has enabled them to amass significant amounts of wealth and influence, de-

veloping associations within the world's foremost power structures in business, science, politics, and religion.

In the research conducted for this book, no clear evidence has been established that any humans have ever set eyes upon an Elder. Their existence has been confirmed only from semi-willing, anonymous members of the vampire community. Even then, most only repeat what they've heard throughout the ages: that major historical events do not occur in the human world without a guiding hand from members of this caste.

Given their high seats of power, Elders no longer engage in blood-hunting activities; their sustenance is provided for by those in their employ. As a result, discussion of defensive tactics against a member of this sect is largely irrelevant. However, the Elders' spheres of influence run deep, and despite never having met or battled a vampire before in your life, it is likely that your existence has already been impacted from the decisions made by this group.

Class Conflict

As in many insular societies, a certain degree of conflict exists among the various undead castes. While all are members of the same biological species, vampires, like humans, exhibit internecine rivalries between their respective groups. Banals often do not interact with Grotesques, believing them to be ineffective or lazy hunters. Seducers look down upon Banals and Grotesques due to their mediocre and low attractiveness. Supremists are largely derisive toward all other classes. These are broad generalizations, however, and should not be taken as sociological dogma for all individual vampires. Being aware of these conflicts, however, may assist you in better understanding your adversary when developing your own strategies for vampire combat.

COMBAT REPORT: CHRISTINE WOLCOTT

Vampire
Williamsburg, Brooklyn

I wander the streets of Brooklyn searching for a building that should not exist. Scheduled for demolition years ago, the tenement I am trying to pinpoint was known to the locals as a squatters' residence, filled with artists and musicians looking for a cheap existence in an expensive city. It is the afternoon of a bright, sweltering August day; the heat and humidity rivals my experience in the Middle East, and almost causes me to abandon my search. Eventually, I discover the shell of a structure once filled with the highest aspirations. The squatters are gone. The hallways echo like a mausoleum. At the request of my interview subject but against my better judgment, I attend the meeting alone.

I enter the building and am immediately met with the distinct scent of decay. The odor grows stronger with each floor as I ascend the staircase in search of my contact. The smell is nearly incapacitating as I reach the top floor. In one corner I see what appears to be a pile of animal carcasses—dogs, cats, and rodents. In the opposite corner sits my contact, Christine Wolcott. Although the loftlike space is cloaked in near-complete darkness, Wolcott covers herself in a large, heavy blanket, obscuring her face from my view. She is seated on a stained twin mattress lying on the floor. Next to the mattress is a single framed photograph, which appears to be Wolcott and another woman who looks so remarkably similar that they could be mistaken for twins. They are both smiling, and stunningly beautiful.

I gingerly seat myself on the floor next to the mattress. Wolcott recedes slightly, not allowing me too close. The odor emanating from her is cloying. I choke back a cough as she begins to speak.

Christine Wolcott: I'm sorry for the smell.

Vampire Combat Manual: It's no bother. Would you mind telling me when you were turned?

CW: Three months ago, but I've been a part of the circle most of my life.

VCM: The circle?

CW: Aficionados of the undead. Goths. Vampire buffs. Just so you know, I'm not some starry-eyed preteen who's read a few romance novels and watched a couple of movies. I was an active member of the community for more than a decade. When I was younger, it was a way to differentiate myself, to be unique. Especially next to Kate.

Wolcott turns her covered head slightly toward the framed picture.

CW: Kate is a few years older than me, but when we were young, she teased that our parents wanted a boy when I was born. I cried to my mother, who told me it wasn't true, but as the years went by, I could sense that Kate was actually telling me the truth. Especially when she began to excel in her life. Kate was their shining star—ballet, track, karate, academics. Everything she touched seemed to come easy. And the easier things came to her, the harder things seemed to get for me. As soon as I set foot in high school, my identity was "Wolcott's kid sister." I know that's not unusual for younger siblings, but this didn't go away, even after she graduated. So instead of trying to be like her, I decided to take a different route. A darker route.

Wolcott pulls the blanket lower over her head, which seems to release a new swell of odors into the room.

CW: People like to ridicule goths—creepy, maudlin, depressing. The truth is we're like everyone else, just trying to fit in. It started with the dark clothes, which my parents despised, but at least tolerated. Then came the piercings. When I started getting into the tattooing, that's when they really flipped. I didn't care, though. To my friends, I was Christine. They didn't give a damn about my sister or what she had done; they just cared about me, and that's exactly what I needed from them.

I started hitting the clubs at sixteen. We were living on Long Island, and I would hitch into the city. I was pretty easy on the eyes back then, and started becoming popular around the scene. After high school graduation, I moved into the city to be closer to the action. My friends and I would spend long nights talking about how wonderful it would be if our obsessions could become reality, if we could actually join the undead. There were some of us who toyed with hokey incantations and alchemy, but we knew it was mostly in jest. Then, six months ago, I met Gregor.

The minute I saw him walk into Labyrinth, his gaze seemed to be fixed on me. Aside from the dark clothing, he didn't seem like your regular goth. Some took him for a poseur, but he was just too damn handsome for anyone to care. I remember that first evening, I would sneak a look toward him throughout the night. He sat at the bar without talking to a soul. He was approached several times by interested parties, both men and women, but he waved them off. Whenever I stole a glance in his direction, he always seemed to already be gazing at me. Still, he didn't approach me once, and left the club without saying a word.

Wolcott shifts under the blanket. Although her limbs are covered by the heavy cloth, I notice her scratching her right forearm.

II. ANATOMY

CW: A month passed, and I didn't see Gregor again. I figured he was just a tourist passing through town for the night, looking to check out the local scene. Then one night at De Sade, I felt a presence behind me. Before I turned around, I knew it was him. Up close, he was even more stunning than how I remembered from afar. He met my eyes again, and I could feel my pulse quicken and my stomach drop into my feet. My ears seemed to close up as if someone turned the volume down on every sound in the entire room, except his voice. More than beautiful, Gregor seemed to radiate with attraction. His face was perfect, free from blemishes, except for a single, two inch-long scar that ran near the bottom of his left ear toward his chin. He introduced himself, took my hand, and we retreated to the back of the club.

We spent the next six hours speaking to no one else. Not only was he handsome; he was powerfully charming, and not in a contrived, transparent way. I wasn't some naïve innocent—men have been trying to talk their way into my pants for years. But Gregor was different. Even though we had just met, he possessed the ability to make me feel like I was the center of the universe, and everything I said was smart and meaningful and worthwhile. His attention was intoxicating and irresistible. Eventually the conversation drifted into my involvement in the scene. Near the end of the night, he posed the question that my friends and I had discussed many times in the past. "If you could, would you become one of them?" My answer was obvious.

For the next month, it seemed that wherever I was for the night, Gregor was there. Orion, Mad Hatter, Hitchcock's; regardless of the place or the night, he would appear, and a similar routine would happen. We would talk for hours, about what, I don't even remember now, but always ending in the same conversation: the possibility of becoming. One evening, as the night was winding down, Gregor gazed hard into my eyes, and told me not to scream. He took the stem of my martini glass and snapped it in two. He held the jagged edge in front of my eyes, brought it to his hand, and cut into his forearm from wrist to elbow. I held my hand to my mouth to stifle a scream, and watched as the wound began closing up on itself before he even finished slicing. He put the shard of glass down, showed me his forearm, unscathed, and flashed a toothy smile. That's when I knew.

VCM: Did he turn you then?

CW: Just the opposite. After that night, he never brought the subject up again; almost like he was rejecting me, as if I wasn't worthy enough. But I certainly wanted to talk about it. Nearly my entire adult life was spent fantasizing about being a part of his world. By the end, I was practically begging to be turned.

One night as I was walking out of Pyramid, something pulled me by the wrist and forced me into an alley adjoining the club. A hand covered my mouth before I could scream. It was Gregor. I hadn't seen him in the club the entire night so I assumed he spent it somewhere else. I know now that he spent the night waiting for me there, like a hunter. Why? I would have offered to be turned in any setting. It was as if he needed it to happen there, in a dark, seedy dead end, between the piles of rotting trash. The last thing I remember is seeing Gregor's eyes roll back as he forced my head to the side and unhinged his mouth. That, and his scar.

I was in my own bed when I awoke. It was still dark, but sunrise was moments away. I immediately thought I dreamed the entire night. Until I reached into my shirt pocket and removed a sliver of paper containing an address and a single word: "Tonight." I began to feel the thirst and, shortly afterward, the pain. Not from the thirst; a throbbing from something much worse.

Wolcott pulls back the blanket, revealing her tattooed right arm. It is covered in boils and open sores, raw and festering. I realize that the odor emanating from Wolcott is from these wounds. I reflexively cover my mouth and nose.

CW: Some kind of allergic reaction with the ink from my tattoos, the wood resins or carbon, maybe trace elements of silver[3]; I'm not exactly sure. All I know is that the pain is agonizing, and the wounds don't heal. The blisters started emerging right after I woke. It was too close to sunrise, so there was nothing I could do but suffer until sunset. When the evening finally arrived, the boils were doubled in size; some were bursting with this rancid fluid. I tried lancing a few of the worst blisters, but that only made things worse. I was in a panic; I had no idea what to do, but I knew Gregor would help me.

I made my way to the address written on the paper—a darkened building in the meatpacking district. I found the single entrance to the building: a blackened steel door with an identification slot that immediately opened when I stepped in front of the doorway. I asked for Gregor, but the guarding eyes peered down at my arm. The fluid from the sores was dripping onto the entranceway. The slot closed, and didn't open again.

I sat in the doorway until nearly daybreak, waiting for Gregor to welcome me in. He never did. I headed home before the sun could rise, crippled with pain from my arm and the thirst. I desperately needed to feed, but I didn't have strength to hunt for a proper meal. I resorted to alternative sources to fill my needs. Gregor didn't mention the effects of feeding on non-humans, so I had no idea until it was too late.

---

3 According to industry experts, there is no known presence of metals in inks commonly used for tattooing. Due to the unavailability of the subject in this report, further research as to the nature of the reaction cannot be conducted.

Wolcott removes the blanket covering her head. It is clear that feeding on the blood of life-forms other than humans has caused her features to deform. She is becoming a Grotesque.

CW: It wasn't supposed to be like this. I was ready; I spent my life preparing to be one of them. Now look at what I've become. But you can help me. I know you can.

VCM: How can . . . ?

Wolcott takes the blanket she has cloaked herself in and unfurls it in my direction, enveloping me in darkness. Thinking the worst, I scramble to retrieve the silver-bladed knife left behind by Nathan Firestone from my bag and brace myself for the impact of Wolcott's body as she attacks. It never comes. I pull the cloth from my head just in time to see her bounding out of the room toward the rooftop staircase, the framed photo in her hand. I begin to give chase in the hope of catching her before she reaches the rooftop, but it is a futile effort. I'm halfway up the stairs when I hear the door to the roof open. An animalistic scream echoes throughout the building. I arrive at the doorway and stare into the blinding heat of the midday sun.

Four feet from the doorway lies what is left of Christine Wolcott—a pile of black ash and remnants of clothing. Beside the remains lies the framed photo. I pick it up. Taped to the underside is an envelope with words handwritten on the exterior. It reads, "To Kate."

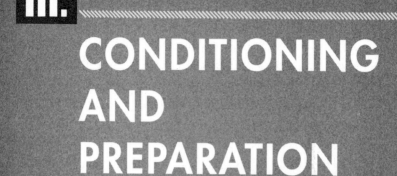

III.

CONDITIONING AND PREPARATION

Our growing softness, our increasing lack of physical fitness, is a menace to our security.

— JOHN F. KENNEDY

SELF-ASSESSMENT

The first step in preparing yourself to effectively counter a vampire's attack is to objectively analyze your tools, the most fundamental of which is your physique. There are three primary physical categories of vampire combatant, known as body somatotypes: ectocombatant, mesocombatant, and endocombatant. Where you personally fall among these three categories depends on your unique physiological shape. Those of you who have read previous analysis work conducted by IUCS in the field of undead combat may be familiar with these somatotypes and the characteristics that define each classification. It is important, however, to re-evaluate these distinct categories under the unique lens of a vampire conflict.

Ectocombatant

Narrow in bone structure and light in musculature, the ectocombatant build presents a unique challenge in vampire combat. Individuals with this physique are the most at risk of all combatant types when battling the undead. At the same time, it is also the least desirable body type to your undead opponent for one simple reason: blood volume.

The quantity of blood coursing through the average adult human equals roughly 7 percent of his or her total body weight. As previously covered in our discussion on vampire anatomy, a standard feeding session can sustain a succubus for up to three days. It is in your opponent's best interests to select an optimal target for its attack—one that can sustain the creature for the maximum amount of time until its next feeding. Much as in any hunting expedition, there are a number of factors at play when selecting prey, but given a choice, a vampire will opt for a larger, "higher volume" target over the slight, thin frame of the ectocombatant.

Those who fall in this class should focus their training primarily on strength-building exercises to boost their musculature, which will greatly enhance their defensive capabilities. At the same time, ectocombatants should be wary of gaining too much extra mass. Remember: You have the benefit of being the least desirable target to this creature; do not undo this advantage. Also note that a thin frame is not necessarily a weak frame; a cyclist, endurance athlete, or mountaineer is clear evidence of this fact.

Once engaged with a member of the undead, the ectocombatant is more vulnerable the longer the duration of a combat engagement. A warrior with this somatotype should focus on refining his technique such that a finishing blow can be executed before he is overpowered by his physically dominating opponent. It would be in the best interests of the ectocombatant to study a martial art that emphasizes technique and leverage over power and strength.

Mesocombatant

The muscular, athletic frame of the mesocombatant makes it exceedingly effective in a combat setting. It is also the most exposed to vampire attack. The meso's larger build means a greater blood volume—highly attractive to a hunting vampire. Additionally, the lower body fat level and increased vascularity (vein prominence) due to thinner skin make it easier for an undead attacker to access a prominent bloodline in the course of its attack. Ironically, the mesocombatant's emphasis on maintaining high levels of physical fitness also make him more at risk, as it is not uncommon for hunting vampires to station themselves near fitness clubs or gymnasiums, hoping to secure an easy target who has just finished an exhausting evening workout.

In both training and combat, the mesocombatant should take extra care to keep not only his physical but his mental state in check. Individuals with a meso build are often physically confident, assertive, and unfortunately more likely to underestimate their undead opponent—particularly one that does not look physically imposing. To do so in a vampire attack is to seal your fate. The undead not only hope their victims miscalculate their vulnerability, they rely on it. By proving to be more resilient than anticipated, a ghoul is often able to mentally break a mesocombatant's will before the outcome of the physical engagement is determined. Combatants with a meso build must always keep in mind that despite their strong and powerful physiques, they are in as much peril as the rest of humanity, if not more so.

Endocombatant

Large in girth and mass, the endocombatant presents an interesting dichotomy in relation to vampire combat. On one hand, their greater body weight means a higher total blood volume, a desirable characteristic for a vampire in search of prey. Individuals with this build are often targeted by a single voracious vampire or the rare hunting pack, as a single large endo may have the blood quantity of two or three average humans.

On the other hand, the larger mass and greater quantity of adipose tissue means a challenge for the vampire in accessing vital arteries during an attack, not to mention the risk of being overwhelmed by an endocombatant's superior size. Largeness with respect to the endocombatant does not necessarily mean obese, just as thinness does not equate to healthfulness in the ectocombatant. Many warriors with the endo build are in good physical condition and are able to train and fight effectively, despite carrying a large amount of weight on their frames.

However, endos do need to objectively assess whether their extra mass is negatively affecting their state of readiness and causing their combat skills to suffer. Should a reduction in weight be deemed advantageous to the endocombatant, the nutritional recommendations provided later in this text may prove useful. Training for this body type should emphasize cardiovascular endurance and stamina, traits which the endo may be lacking in an engagement with the undead.

PHYSICAL CONDITIONING

In our discussion on anatomy, we emphasized the fact that in a combat engagement with a vampire, you will be facing an opponent that is physically superior compared to any human opponent you have ever encountered. Why, then, you may wonder, should you even bother with physical conditioning? Why not emphasize strategy and combat techniques instead, given the fact that you will always be at a physiological disadvantage and rarely be able to match your opponent in athletic prowess?

While it is absolutely true that the techniques and strategies you employ in battle will ultimately determine your success in vampire combat, your level of conditioning is what provides the opportunity to deliver these techniques at the precise moment to ensure victory. Both technique and conditioning are necessities in battling a bloodthirsty ghoul—perfecting one without the other will doom you to failure.

Let us also make this point clear: We are not discussing a gentlemanly match of fisticuffs or a rule-bound grappling bout. Most vampire engagements last no more than a few minutes, and, like most assaults, are brutal, vicious, and utterly exhausting. The window of opportunity you have to survive the attack and neutralize your opponent is already slim; your level of conditioning can help widen that gap. The other detail to reemphasize is that as a human being, you have the ability to continue to improve your athleticism regardless of your age or current level of fitness. Your undead opponent, on the other hand, is unable to improve its physical assets with additional exercise.

When it comes to what type of conditioning you should focus on, there are many varieties of exercise you can employ to help your overall fitness level. We will concentrate our discussion, however, on activities that will explicitly improve your chances in vampire combat.

Calisthenics

A pervasive myth about physical fitness is that elaborate machines and expensive facilities are required to develop a healthy physique. In fact, most individuals can achieve outstanding results simply by utilizing exercises that were learned in grade school. There is a reason why despite a plethora of convoluted and obscure training methods that emerge year after year, basic calisthenics exercises are still used as a part of the training regimens of professional athletes, soldiers, and fighters.

Push-ups, pull-ups, squats, crunches, and jumping jacks are all exercises that require no equipment other than one's own body weight and can produce a combat-ready physique, particularly for those who are new to conditioning or have not maintained a regular exercise routine. It is no coincidence that most military forces around the world focus on calisthenics to mold average civilians into a hardened fighting force. A simple circuit of calisthenics, performed one after the other with little rest between movements, can be an excellent starting point for the unconditioned vampire combatant.

Due to the familiarity most individuals have with these common exercises, we will not delve into the basic instructions required for each of these movements. However, there are three key points worth noting when performing a routine based on calisthenics.

I. Push Your Body—When performing exercises that utilize gravity and your body weight as the oppositional forces, it is easy to lull yourself into a lackadaisical routine. It should go without saying that the amount of effort you apply to each activity is directly corre-lated to the benefit gained from the exercise. When executing each individual movement, perform an ap-propriate number of repetitions in which the final few are nearly impossible to complete.

2. **Move with Purpose**—Always keep in mind that you are training with a very specific objective—to save your own life in the small window of opportunity available during a vampire attack. Move with haste between each exercise, and execute each movement focusing on your ultimate intention: to survive.

3. **Visualize Your Battle**—It is easy to become distracted while performing any exercise routine, calisthenics in particular. You may have witnessed this your-self—an individual in the gym with good inten-tions, roaming about from machine to machine like a mindless zombie. In order to help retain your focus and attention span, visualize the relevance of your exercises to vampire combat. A push-up is no longer a push-up, but rather a means of keeping gnashing fangs a safe distance away. Not only does this help maintain your focus, it can also calm your senses in an actual combat setting, having already addressed the possible scenario successfully in your mind. Although we are discussing visualization in this particular section on calisthenics, it is a tech-nique that should be employed in all the exercises covered.

Weight Training

Once thought to be limited to the realm of muscle-bound bodybuilders and barrel-chested power lifters, research now shows that weight-bearing resistance exercises not only improve an individual's musculature, they can also strengthen the supporting tendons, ligaments, and even the structural density of the skeletal system—important benefits when battling a physically superior opponent. Performed using a method we will discuss shortly, weight training can also enhance a combatant's cardiovascular threshold, a critical factor in hand-to-hand combat.

Just as there are body-weight exercises that emphasize specific regions of the body, there are weight-lifting movements that can focus on the smallest muscle groups, such as the biceps and triceps muscles in the arms. While enhancing these small muscles may be important to some for the sake of vanity, keep in mind that your training objective is very different from the ordinary gym rat. For this reason, the weight-training movements we recommend are ones that work several muscle groups in unison. Not only does this maximize your time spent in training, it helps mimic the coordination that may be required of you in times of battle and minimizes the amount of equipment necessary to complete your routine.

Rather than describe the execution of these movements in detail, we will describe the applicability of each exercise specific to its relation to vampire combat so that you can understand their applicability in your training regimen.

BENCH PRESSES

Primary Muscles Targeted:
Pectorals (Chest), Deltoids
(Shoulders), Triceps (Arms)

Combat Applicability: As we
will discuss in the section
on Combat Strategies and
Techniques, a determining factor in your survival
will be your ability to keep your attacker at bay long
enough to mount an effective counterstrike. As one of
the favored targets of a vampire is the human neck,
your ability to defend your upper torso and head region will be critical to your success. Improving your
upper body strength will enhance your defensive capabilities, and there are few more effective upper
body exercises than the weighted bench press. This
movement targets all the muscles that you will be
forcefully using in your upper body should you come
face to face with a ravenous succubus.

SHOULDER PRESSES

Primary Muscles Targeted: Deltoids
(Shoulders), Triceps (Arms)

Combat Applicability: The ability to
thrust a neutralizing stake into the
heart not only depends on your skill in
pinpointing this small target while in
motion, but also your ability to drive
your weapon through clothing, flesh,
and bone. Power in your shoulders and

arms is critical to delivering a combat-ending blow. As you often do not have the opportunity to deliver a follow-up strike, ensure you have the strength to make the first one count. The shoulder press is not only successful at developing the muscles you will utilize to thrust and stab at your opponent, it also helps strengthen the joints and ligaments connecting the shoulder itself, which is susceptible to tearing and damage due to the fragile nature of its ball-and-socket design in the human body

SQUATS/DEAD LIFTS

Primary Muscles Targeted: Gluteus Maximus, Quadriceps (Fronts of Legs), Hamstrings (Backs of Legs)

Combat Applicability: The squat and the dead lift comprise two of the three movements often called the holy trinity of exercises in powerlifting, the third being the aforementioned bench press. The reason is simple. With these three exercises, you can target most of the major muscle groups in the body while also building

tremendous functional strength. An unfortunate mistake many individuals make is ignoring their lower body and focusing on the more prominent muscles on top due to vanity. Do not make the same error. The legs form the powerful foundation for your overall balance and act as the launching point for both your defensive maneuvers and offensive counterattacks. If your foundation is weak, your entire body will suffer.

BENT ROWS

Primary Muscles Targeted: Latissimus Dorsi (Back), Biceps (Arms), Forearms

Combat Applicability: A strenuous exercise that develops the other large muscle group on the upper body—the latissimus dorsi— bent-over rows also have the compound effect of building your biceps, forearms, and grip strength. In vampire combat, each of these muscle groups plays an essential role in undead defense and vampire neutralization. The pulling motion utilized in this exercise also replicates the withdrawing of your weapon from an opponent's body. As you may find yourself fending off a hostile undead opponent looking to bring you to the ground, strengthening the lower back region also prevents unwarranted stress and unforeseen injury to this delicate area.

High-Intensity Interval Training (HIIT)

Anthropological research has found that the human body has evolved to become an efficient mobile specimen. We, as humans, are effectively born to run. What we lack in initial acceleration and overall speed we make up for in endurance and stamina, with early humans able to literally "run down" their targeted prey. In the case of vampire combat, humans are on the unfortunate side of the hunt. The combat applicability of running during an undead encounter is often misunderstood. What is the point, you may ask, of trying to outdistance a creature that can inevitably overcome you? Those who question the value of this exercise are missing the larger point.

The goal of running is not so that, at some point, you will be able to outrun your undead attacker in a footrace. Given what is known about the speed of the average vampire at maximum acceleration, we know this to be a futile venture. Running, however, can build the stamina required to sustain your endurance levels during an intense combat encounter. A unique type of cardiovascular fortitude is required in vampire combat—one that begins at a moment's notice and is sustained at maximum levels for a brief period of time. You can build this type of endurance by being intelligent about your methods and running smarter, not harder. One such method of running smarter is high intensity interval training (HIIT).

Although there are a variety of types of HIIT methods—Tabata Protocols, Turbulence Training, the Little Method—the basic premise is similar: perform an exercise at the highest intensity for a short duration, alternating with a shorter rest period. The routine ends once you have completed this sequence for a set number of repetitions. The following routine is a typical endurance session using the Tabata Method of HIIT.

The Tabata Method

- 3-Minute Jog (Warm-up)
- 20-Second Sprint (Maximum speed)
- 10-Second Rest (Walking pace)
- Repeat for 8-10 cycles

The fitness benefits claimed by HIIT methods are significant: decreases in body fat, increases in lean muscle tissue and aerobic capacity, and a pronounced calorie-burning effect long after your workout has ended, not to mention that the entire routine can be completed in less than ten minutes. In relation to undead combat, HIIT enables you to replicate the short, frenetic bursts of energy required to fend off a ravenous vampire during its attack. These workouts, however, can be extremely intense for the untrained individual. During the sprint segment of the Tabata Method, you should be running at top speed, as if your life hangs in the balance—which, in effect, it does.

Circuit Training

As important as the specific exercises that comprise your training regimen is the manner in which you perform them. Many people who devote time to fitness often boast of spending hours in the gym completing an intricate variety of movements. What they fail to realize is that a majority of this time is spent not in training, but rather socializing. Any individual who spends more than ninety minutes completing their entire exercise routine is working themselves into the ground or more likely spending their time inefficiently, wasting long stretches in a resting state.

Always keep in mind that the goal of your regimen is to prepare you against the onslaught from a bloodthirsty attacker. Your routine should replicate the brevity and intensity of such an encounter. One of the keys to improving your cardiovascular fitness level is ensuring that your heart rate is kept elevated for the entire duration of your training session. An effective workout sequence can be created by combining a variety of exercises that address both the lower and upper half of the body in alternating patterns, and completed in less than one hour.

The following is an excellent starting routine that requires no specialized equipment. Once a single circuit becomes easy to complete, additional sequences should be added to the routine, with no rest between each individual exercise and a minute of rest between completed sequences.

Vampire Fundamental Conditioning Circuit (VFCC)

- 5 Tabata Protocols
- 50 Push-ups
- 50 Squats (Body weight)
- 50 Jumping Jacks
- 50 Crunches
- 50 Squats (Body weight)

Should you have the access to free weights and the desire to incorporate them into your routine, sample the following weighted conditioning circuit. For the weight-bearing exercises, choose poundage that is challenging enough to fully complete the required number of repetitions, albeit with great difficulty.

Vampire Weighted Conditioning Circuit (VWCC)

- 10 Tabata Protocols
- 20 Squats
- 20 Bent Rows
- 20 Bench Presses
- 20 Dead Lifts
- 20 Shoulder Presses

Combat Exercises

Standard calisthenics, cardiovascular exercise, and weight training will improve your overall fitness, but exercises that improve conditioning while simultaneously enhancing your combat effectiveness are ideal when preparing for battle. To accomplish both, you will need to incorporate exercises that replicate similar movements you will perform in an undead engagement. While you can create your own exercises, we have developed a series of movements that replicate actions you may perform during a vampire attack.

JOHN HENRYS An excellent exercise to develop your arm and back strength and improve your staking and targeting abilities, John Henrys replicate the act of swinging forcibly downward into your opponent and striking a small target. Using a small sledgehammer (or, if unavailable, a household hammer) and an automobile tire, mark an area of the tire for your swing. Hold the tool above your head, and bring it down heavily onto your target, striking it with all your might. Complete ten repetitions, then re-peat with the opposite hand. Increase the number of repetitions or weight of the hammer as the movements become easier. Do not overlook training with your weaker, non-dominant hand. In combat, it is possible that your strong arm may become disabled. Developing

ambidexterity in your offensive strikes will make you a much more fearsome and well-rounded combatant.

DEFENDER SQUATS This is a variation of the archetypal squat, with the exception of using a human partner to add weight to your movement rather than a barbell. In a standing position, have a training partner straddle your back and secure his arms around your neck. With your back straight, squat down until your upper thighs are parallel to the ground, and push back up until your legs are nearly straight. Keep continuous pressure on your thigh muscles by keeping your knees bent at the top of the technique. This movement not only provides the physical benefits of the squat exercise, it replicates a possible scenario where your opponent will attack from the rear, back-mounted position. Becoming accustomed to the feeling of someone on your back will make it less likely for you to panic should you find yourself in such a predicament.

GRIM REAPERS Replicating the heavy, swinging motions required when using a bladed weapon to maim or decapitate your undead opponent, take a medicine ball (or, if unavailable, a ten- to fifteen-pound sandbag) in both hands and raise it overhead. Using primarily your back muscles, slam the ball down onto the ground in front of you. Repeat for ten repetitions. This forceful technique can also help develop flexibility and range of motion in your shoulders, a great benefit when you find yourself repeatedly swinging your weapon at your undead adversary.

CLAIM JUMPERS This unusual exercise simulates the equally unique experience of having to drive a wooden stake into the heart of an undead opponent. Holding a wooden dowel similar in size and shape to the weapon you would use in combat, lie on a soft surface (preferably sand or loose dirt). Raise your weapon-bearing hand high in the air while reclining on the elbow of the opposite arm. Bring the weapon down forcefully, driving it into the earth as deep as you can manage. Repeat this movement for 15-20 repetitions. Switch your position, and perform the same movement with the alternate hand. Attempt to strike the same location with each repetition in order to develop better hand-eye coordination and precision in your strikes.

MARTIAL ARTS TRAINING

A question often posed by those who look to prepare themselves for undead battle is, "What is the best combat style to defend against a vampire attack?" The answer to this query is a simple one—any style and no style. While this response may sound like an ambiguous, philosophical koan, it is not. Any martial arts style will teach you fundamental principles of combat that are valuable in any engagement against an attacking opponent, vampiric or otherwise. Timing, range, distance, and footwork are all basic concepts that you will learn when you embark on any martial arts training. No martial arts style is ideal due to the fact that none were originally developed to prepare a human opponent for the intricacies specific to vampire combat.

Martial arts are generally separated into two categories: hard arts and soft arts. Hard arts are used to describe those styles that focus on utilizing forceful blows to halt an oncoming opponent, such as strikes incorporating the hands, feet, knees, and elbows. Examples of hard arts include most of the traditional karate and kung fu styles as well as Muay Thai kickboxing, Israeli Krav Maga, and Western boxing. Soft arts, on the other hand, are those arts that often divert or misdirect the attacker's strength and momentum to gain the upper hand while using the minimal amount of force necessary to subdue your opponent. In general, the soft arts are more suited to vampire combat due to the fact that not only are most strikes ineffective against this particular adversary, but you will also almost always find yourself the physically lesser of the two combatants in an undead engagement, and as a result cannot rely on superior strength or power to overcome your attacker.

Equally important to note is the fact no single combat

style can provide all the elements required to fend off an attacking vampire. A much better martial strategy is to study a variety of different arts based on the strengths and vulnerabilities detailed earlier regarding your opponent, emphasizing elements in each art that can provide you an advantage in undead combat. There are also some particular combat styles that have proven useful to experienced survivors of vampire attack.

Judo

Literally translated as "the gentle way," judo was created in the late 1800s by Dr. Jigoro Kano, who grew up in Japan as a weak and frail child. Even into adulthood, Dr. Kano weighed no more than one hundred pounds. The forefather to many other grappling styles, judo's primary goal is to subdue your opponent with a throw or takedown. While the art also incorporates such techniques

as submission holds and chokes, the emphasis is on using the proper technique to fling your opponent to the ground.

Against a vampire, the knowledge afforded by the study of judo will assist you greatly in being able to use balance, anatomy, and weight distribution to set up your opponent for a throw. Once on the ground, you can decide whether to disengage from your opponent and escape, or initiate a neutralizing counterattack.

The trained judo artist, or judoka, must also exhibit some

caution when using this art against an attacking vampire. A judo throw per se will not be enough to subdue or deter a bloodthirsty vampire. Care must be taken not to underestimate the strength and power of your opponent based on external appearances, as a vampire's looks are almost always deceiving. The judoka also must be aware that a creature's goal is not to fight its prey, but to feed upon it. Setting up a throw may place the vampire in a position close to the judo player's veins and arteries, which the creature may exploit with an unexpected counterattack.

Brazilian Jiu-Jitsu

As a young boy in Brazil, Hélio Gracie sat and watched his larger, fitter brothers practicing a traditional form of judo taught to them by Mitsuyo Maeda, a Japanese family friend. Considered too weak in physical constitution to train, Gracie watched for years as his brothers performed the movements they were taught. As he studied the techniques being performed, young Hélio made mental adjustments to the movements so that someone smaller and weaker such as himself could execute them just as well without needing to rely on

strength or power. These adjustments and the continuous refinement of the original Japanese techniques have become what is commonly known throughout the world today as Brazilian jiu-jitsu (BJJ). While the art has continued to develop and evolve over the years, the style's fundamental concept has remained the same: Technique, strategy, and leverage can defeat size, power, and strength.

In vampire combat, the greatest strength of Brazilian jiu-jitsu is the ability of the skilled BJJ player to defend himself on the ground. Once any combat engagement ends up with both combatants on the ground as opposed to standing, many obvious physical advantages are neutralized to a certain degree. Countless videos exist of seemingly thin and weak BJJ artists defeating much larger and stronger opponents. And in an engagement with the undead, it is almost a given that you will be the weaker combatant.

Although Brazilian jiu-jitsu provides an excellent combat foundation against the undead, there are issues that the BJJ practitioner must be wary of as well. Although ground fighting is an excellent skill to possess against a vampire, remaining entangled with the undead on the ground for an extended period of time is still not an optimal situation. The longer you are engaged with the creature, the more likely it is that the vampire will prevail.. The BJJ player must also be careful with utilizing techniques that may not elicit the desired response from an undead opponent, specifically choking techniques that cut the flow of oxygen to the brain. In a human opponent, a lack of oxygenated blood flow will result in loss of consciousness in seconds. Against a vampire, such techniques are altogether ineffective, since oxygen is not required by the creature to survive. The most effective use of BJJ against the undead is to combine the art's techniques with a terminating strike to the susceptible vampire heart.

III. CONDITIONING AND PREPARATION

Wrestling

An ancient form of physical combat, yet not ordinarily considered a "martial art," wrestling has a history that extends back more than 15,000 years and was the primary sport of the original Greek Olympics. Variations of the art can be found in ancient Babylonia, Egypt, Greece, China, and Rome. Modern wrestling disciplines are now considered more of a sport and practiced throughout the United States at the middle school, high school, and collegiate level. The two best-known forms are Greco-Roman, which does not allow techniques below the waist, and freestyle, which permits the use of the legs in offense and defense. Other lesser known but equally effective styles include catch wrestling and folk-style wrestling, which incorporate submission-style techniques similar to those seen in jiu-jitsu and judo.

The experienced wrestler has a set of skills that can prove extremely valuable against an attacking ghoul, both in a defensive and offensive sense. One of the proficiencies possessed by a wrestling practitioner is what is known as a "takedown defense"—the ability to defend against an opponent that wants to take you off your feet. In a vampire engagement, a primary tactic used by the undead is to bring their prey to the ground where the victim can be immobilized and easily drained of blood. Wrestling provides the necessary skills to prevent such takedowns from occurring. Additionally, conditioning practices for wrestling have a reputation for being exceptionally taxing, perfect preparation for an undead engagement, where your physical and mental stamina will be pushed to their limits.

The wrestler also needs to be acutely aware of the limitations of his art. Due to wrestling's emphasis on grappling your opponent to the ground, wrestlers often utilize strength and power to grind down their opponent's defenses. Against an attacking ghoul, such a war of attrition will work to the vampire's benefit. The wrestler must also change his mindset from participating in an athletic event where the objective is to pin your opponent's shoulders to the mat, to a real-world combat scenario where the objective is to exterminate your attacker and emerge unharmed.

Sambo

A relatively unknown but growing martial art, sambo has its origins in Russia, where its name is an acronym for the Russian term *samooborona bez oruzhiya*, literally meaning "self-defense without weapons." Like Brazilian jiu-jitsu, sambo's roots can be found in Japanese judo, one of the developers of the art having lived in Japan and studied directly under Dr. Kano. As the art developed, its techniques evolved from those

requiring great strength to ones focused on movement and strategy. This evolution was intentional, as Victor Spiridonov, one of the founders of sambo, suffered a bayonet wound in World War I, leaving him without the use of his left arm. Spiridonov realized that he would enter every combat engagement at a significant bodily disadvantage, and developed sambo so that even those who were not as physically capable could still defeat their challengers.

In vampire combat, the sambo fighter can leverage these strategy-based techniques to outmaneuver a faster, stronger undead adversary. The sambo uniform itself—a kimono-like top combined with short pants and shoes—is a very practical outfit in which to train for vampire defense. The jacket enables the sambo player to grab the collar and sleeves, much like you can grab the creature's attire. Incorporating footwear also replicates a street encounter with a vampire, where you will be wearing shoes on your feet. Sambo is also known for its sophisticated leg-locking techniques, which can be used to great advantage to immobilize an attacking vampire while keeping your own body out of harm's way.

Much like in the other grappling arts discussed, the samboist must be wary of using submission techniques against an opponent who cannot be forced to submit. Even the vicious leg techniques mentioned previously should be used with the caveat that leg locks will not cause a vampire a considerable amount of discomfort due to its higher pain tolerance. They can, however, prevent an attacking ghoul from scrambling toward your throat, looking to commence its feeding session.

Kali

Very few martial arts in the world today incorporate the use of weapons as thoroughly as in the art of Kali. Whereas other styles limit the study of armaments only to the most

advanced students, Kali's primary focus is developing skill in both impact (stick) and edged (knife) weapons from the onset of training. Originating in the Philippines, a society with an active blade culture and where knife use is a part of daily life, Kali was developed during intertribal warfare among the indigenous peoples of the various Philippine Islands, which is why, depending on the landmass, the names of this martial art will vary from Kali to Escrima to Arnis.

The greatest advantage the Kali practitioner, or Kalista, brings to vampire combat is his extensive skill with edged weapons against the humanoid torso. As you already have learned, a primary method to emerge victorious against an attacking bloodsucker is use of a proper armament directed to a precise target on your opponent. The study of Kali will assist you greatly in the development of this level of precision and enable you to become familiar with using close-combat hand weapons during a vampire engagement. Advanced Kali practitioners also study the use of improvised weapons extensively in the event that a proper combat blade is unavailable. An understanding of makeshift implements can be invaluable in a vampire engagement, in which you may likely be unprepared for sudden and violent assault.

III. CONDITIONING AND PREPARATION

Kalistas must also be cognizant of their art's limitations against the vampire species. Although Kali emphasizes edged weapons training, many of the strikes utilize a slashing pattern, which follows a series of attack angles targeting a variety of regions on the body. A slicing cut made with an edged weapon can be devastating against a human opponent. Against an undead attacker with a superior healing ability, these types of strikes are much less destructive, with most laceration wounds healing rapidly on the vampire's flesh. In preparing for undead combat, the Kali practitioner needs to focus on aggressive thrusting attacks. A single, well-placed blow to the creature's heart by a trained Kalista will end the battle instantaneously.

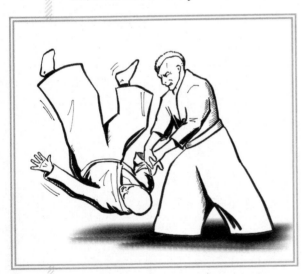

Aikido

Translated as "the way of unifying life energy," aikido's primary martial objective is to divert and redirect an opponent's energy force, rather than confront it with an oppositional counterforce. Another art where size and strength are less important than proper application of technique, aikido teaches practitioners to develop an acute sensitivity to body motion, movement, and energy direction to execute their techniques.

Aikido has been denigrated in certain martial arts circles as an art that is ineffective during an actual combat situation.

While the veracity of this claim can be argued, it is clear aikido practitioners bring a valuable skill to vampire combat. The aikido player is at his best when confronting a raging vampire in a blitz-type attack. The undisciplined charging of a thirsty ghoul plays right into the aikidoist's hands, and is precisely the type of attack for which this art prepares its students. The skilled aikido stylist can use the uncontrolled fury of a stampeding bloodsucker to deflect its energy into a powerful throw. Additionally, this particular martial art places a great emphasis on a relaxed mental and physical state even under dramatic levels of duress, such as when an attacker wants to drain your body of its life force. Morihei Ueshiba, the founder of aikido, once remarked that a practitioner "must be willing to receive 99% of an opponent's attack and stare death in the face." Against a bloodthirsty vampire, death is exactly what you will be facing.

As with other martial arts, aikido is not without its shortcomings in vampire combat, the most significant liability being the time required to gain proficiency in its techniques. More so than in most other martial arts, Aikido practitioners must devote a considerable amount of time and dedication in order to achieve even a modicum of skill, a requirement that many busy individuals simply cannot meet. The techniques themselves also seem to work best against an undisciplined, charging vampire; should he encounter a ghoul that takes a more measured approach in its attack, the aikidoist may have difficulty executing his techniques. Finally, the art of aikido is much more harmonious than all other arts mentioned. The founder's intention was to create an art that can provide defense, but also protect the attacker from serious injury. This type of courtesy, while gracious in nature, is not particularly helpful against an attacker looking at you as its next meal.

III. CONDITIONING AND PREPARATION

Although we have covered a handful of martial arts, there are many more combat styles that provide similar benefits in case of a vampire assault, shuai jiao, hapkido, kenjutsu, and luta livre among them. The intention was not to spotlight one particular art as better than any other, but to provide additional detail on styles that have a ubiquitous enough presence that individuals can locate a training academy with relative ease. Should you decide to study a martial art with the primary objective of gaining an advantage over an attacker looking to drain your blood, ask yourself the following questions about the prospective style:

1. Does the martial art focus on striking or grappling as the primary strategy?

2. Do speed and strength factor heavily into successful execution of the techniques?

3. Can an individual skilled in this art defeat a larger or stronger opponent?

4. How long must you train to become moderately proficient in the art?

Perhaps what is most important is the fact that, as most martial artists come to realize, it is not the art itself, but the practitioner that makes it most effective in combat. There is no one perfect martial style for a vampire engagement, or any type of combat for that matter. It is a blend of styles, combined with the skill and dedication of the artist, that can enable humans to prevail against the undead.

COMBAT REPORT: JAMES CARVER

Martial Artist
Costa Mesa, California

Like most of the subjects I've met for this project, James Carver insists on meeting at an outdoor location in broad daylight. We settle in for brunch at a street-side café. As is often the case in Southern California, the weather is near perfect. The cloudless sky allows the sun's rays to warm the patio table where we both sit. Despite the glorious weather, Carver has a look of melancholy on his face; a mixture of fear and regret for the events he is about to divulge.

James Carver: They call them "challenge matches," or "dojo storms." Very popular decades ago when martial artists were still looking to prove how dominant their own style of combat was. A martial artist would approach the instructor at a rival academy and challenge an individual to a match, which often would take place minutes later on the mats. These matches evolved into the sport of mixed martial arts that you see today, which also pretty much eliminated the need for these types of confrontations. People learned which styles were best for certain situations and which were not, and most fighters no longer had anything to prove. That's why when I saw it happening before my eyes, I could hardly believe it; especially considering the challenger who entered the academy.

It was almost ten o'clock in the evening, and Professor Suares was finishing up instructing a late advanced class, purple belt rank and higher. Three young men walked in the door, clad in mostly black, wearing long dark overcoats and military-style combat boots. They looked ridiculous and unsettling at the same time; ridiculous in that they looked as cliché as you could possibly imagine, right out of central casting for "miserable delinquents." Unsettling in that it was clear they didn't give a damn what anyone thought. Two were average in height and build, but the third looked tired and frail, like he could be knocked sideways by a gust of wind. None of them looked older than twenty-five. Without saying a word to the receptionist, one stood by the door while the two others stepped directly onto the mats in their boots, an intentionally disrespectful act. The thin one then issued the challenge to the professor. The class nearly erupted in laughter, thinking it was some kind of stunt put on by Suares, who loved his practical jokes. It was funny until a student put his hands on the challenger.

Billy, a purple belt who worked part-time at the academy, patted the challenger's shoulder gently to politely usher him off the mat. With blinding speed, the challenger grabbed Billy by the throat and hurled him into the wall. The impact knocked Billy unconscious, his body remaining suspended in the drywall. Chris, a brown belt and one of the more experienced students, ran over and tried to grab the challenger, who threw him into the wall next to Billy, in almost the exact same position. It was like staring at two cartoon characters who'd just been outsmarted by a roadrunner. It would have been comical to me if I weren't scared out of my mind.

The professor told reception to call the police, which is when the individual by the door tore the phone line out of the wall. The challenger then grabbed Billy again by the throat and pulled him free of the wall, still unconscious. "Fight, or everyone here will suffer." Suares put his hands up in a calming gesture and said he would accept the challenge under one condition—win or lose, no further harm was to come to any of the students. The challenger released Billy and immediately squared off with the professor. They began to circle, the challenger staring dead-eyed at the professor. Suares moved slowly and methodically while he watched the challenger's movements. In his youth, the professor was an impressive competitor and rumored to have fought in unsanctioned *vale tudo*[4] matches in Brazil. But that was many years ago.

The professor grabbed hold of the challenger with judo grips: one hand gripping the challenger's jacket collar and the other his opposite sleeve. The challenger reached up with his hand toward the professor's shoulder and tore the sleeve clean off his *gi* uniform. The fabric of a heavyweight *gi* is a dense, multi-weaved cotton, tough and thick, like burlap. The challenger ripped it from the seams like it was tissue paper. Blood ran down the professor's arm where the challenger's nails cut into his flesh as he tore the fabric. The sight of the blood caused a noticeable reaction from both the challenger and his entourage. The professor looked down at his arm, and then at the challenger for a moment, and then back down at the wound. He damped the blood with his sleeve and continued to fight.

The professor probably outweighed his opponent by more than forty pounds, and it seemed he wanted to use that size advantage to end the match as quickly as possible. He sprung at the legs of the challenger, brought him crashing down to the mat, and climbed onto his back, a very bad position against an expert in ground fighting. When the class saw the professor take his back, many of us breathed a sigh of relief, knowing that the end of this disturbing encounter was near. Sure enough, the professor secured a stranglehold known as the rear-naked choke around the neck of the challenger and began to squeeze.

An average adult caught in such a submission hold lasts no more than ten seconds before he passes out. The arm closes

---

4 Vale Tudo: "anything goes" in Portuguese, combat matches fought with very few rules.

III. CONDITIONING AND PREPARATION

off the circulation in the carotid arteries running down both sides of the neck, blocking the flow of blood to the brain and forcing the person to either submit or lose consciousness. The professor has probably finished opponents in this submission thousands of times in his life. He squeezed the neck of the challenger for at least two minutes, with no visible effect. Even more bizarre, the challenger wasn't making the slightest attempt at escaping the hold. He wasn't pulling at Suares's arms or wrists, the standard defense tactic. He simply lay there with his hands folded in his lap as the professor squeezed tighter and tighter. Eventually the challenger got to his feet, bent downward, and, with the professor still on his back, ran into the academy wall headfirst, slamming both of their skulls through it. The professor fell off the challenger's back and stood, visibly dazed. The challenger stood up as well, completely unfazed. He was smiling. I looked into the professor's eyes, and what flashed in them was a look I'd never seen in all my years training with him: a look of genuine fear.

That look lasted only a few seconds. What immediately took its place was an appearance of composure, almost as if the professor had a vision, realizing precisely what he needed to do against this challenger. He reached up to the wound on his shoulder and pulled at it slightly, causing a new stream of blood to emerge from the cut. The challenger's eyes widened, and his mouth went slightly agape. Blood ran down the length of the professor's arm, dripping onto the mat. The challenger charged in a frenzy. The professor stepped nimbly to the side and squared off against his visibly angered opponent. They fought this way for several minutes, running the length of the academy—the challenger rushing in and swinging wildly, the professor adeptly shifting and moving his body weight, diverting the force of the attack. Rather than trying to match his opponent's strength and aggression, the professor did the polar opposite. It looked like the challenger was struggling against an empty uniform.

As they continued to fight, they ended up close to the plate-glass window of the academy entrance. The challenger lunged, and the professor executed a basic leg trip that brought both of them to the ground again. It was clear this time that the strategy was going to be different. The professor snaked both of his legs around one of the challenger's biceps. Using both of his arms to secure the challenger's other free arm, the professor pulled the limbs apart, splaying the challenger in a crucifix-type position. With his arms pinned and the full weight of the professor pressing him into the mat, the challenger struggled to rise to his feet. The more he struggled, the tighter the professor held him. As the challenger continued to twist, the professor turned his head and whispered to the challenger, *"Podemos ficar assim até o amanhecer."* [5] His associates ran onto the mat when they heard the professor, but a look from the challenger froze them in their tracks. He then raised his hand slightly, and tapped on the mat once. Professor Suares released the hold. The challenger rose to his feet, and the men exited the academy without another word.

We rushed to the professor's side to tend to his injury, and another student began to call the police. Professor stopped him and, after ensuring that Billy and Chris were okay, directed us to sit on the mat and listen to him closely. He instructed all of us not to mention that night to anyone, friends or family. "You are my senior students. If you respect me and this school, you will keep what happened here tonight between us."

Two months after this incident, there was a fire at the academy. The school was burned to the ground. Investigators

---

5 Portuguese: "We can stay this way until sunrise."

said it was arson, and ultimately blamed it on the professor, attributing it to insurance fraud. Anyone who knew Suares would know that couldn't be the case. That place was his life. Unfortunately, the professor wasn't around to defend himself from the accusation. He disappeared the day after the fire.

Vampire Combat Manual: If Suares asked you to remain silent, why disclose this now?

JC: My commitment was to my professor. With him gone, the best thing I can do for him now is to make sure what happened that night doesn't happen to another academy. A few weeks ago, a friend of mine from Texas told me about this incident at his school—three men entering in the evening and issuing a challenge to the instructor. He wasn't as skilled as Professor Suares.

Carver looks at his hands, and then upward toward the bright light of the noonday sun.

JC: We were all basking in the glow of the professor's triumph that night, but Suares knew something none of us did. He didn't win that fight. The moment they set foot into our academy and manhandled his students, I think the professor realized the type of opponent he was facing. I think he knew he had already lost. But that didn't matter. He didn't fight for his business, his ego or reputation, or even some antiquated notion of honor. He fought that night simply to make sure that his students were safe.

He fought for us.

PSYCHOLOGICAL PREPARATION

While the primary focus of this text is to prepare you physically for an impending vampire attack, your opponent may also wage an intense psychological battle during your engagement. This is particularly true if the creature is a member of the Seducer vampire sect, feels at risk of being defeated, or simply looks to entertain itself by manipulating its opponent prior to finishing its attack, much like a feline will toy with its prey prior to killing it.

As intense as a physical confrontation can be against the undead, a mental assault can be just as traumatic. Members of the undead who are adept at using psychological tactics against their opponents often spend decades researching, studying, and analyzing the human psyche in order to find the optimal way to subdue their victims merely by conversing with them. Many will employ techniques used by the medical community, such as psychotherapy, neurolinguistic programming (NLP), and psychiatric training in order to achieve their objective. Some will go to great lengths to gain advanced proficiency in these skills, obtaining doctorate-level educations in these fields simply to become expert manipulators of the human condition. Just as you need to condition your body to withstand a vampire's physical assault, you must steel your mind in order not to fall victim to its cerebral attack. Following are recommendations to prepare your mental state prior to and during an undead engagement.

Trust Your Instincts—A difficult aspect of mentally preparing for a vampire attack is the fact that you could live your entire life without encountering one.

III. CONDITIONING AND PREPARATION

It is imperative, however, that you maintain an awareness of your surroundings, operating under the probability that you may someday be attacked. This low level of readiness can enhance your instincts in recognizing a potentially hazardous situation in advance. Should your instincts signal that a setting feels perilous for no apparent reason, take note. You may also experience moments throughout life where you feel the eyes of some unknown and unseen entity upon you. Although there are detractors of the "staring effect" and research continues into this phenomenon, some believe that human beings can tap into something akin to a sixth sense of being observed. This sensation seems to grow particularly acute if the staring entity has negative or violent intentions associated with its gaze. While this phenomenon is yet to be confirmed by the scientific community, err on the side of caution and take heed of these feelings should you experience them.

Do Not Speak—Should you find yourself in the midst of a vampire attack, do not attempt to engage your opponent in any type of conversation or discourse. Remember that despite its humanoid appearance, the vampire's intentions are focused solely on obtaining nourishment; any attempt to converse with your adversary provides it an opportunity to launch a psychological assault in the hopes of achieving its objective. The temptation to speak to a member of the undead is difficult to resist for many, as curiosity often trumps common sense. Individuals with higher intelligence or impressive educational pedigrees may also feel capable of handling themselves against what they may feel is an equal or inferior intellect. Do not fall into this trap. Regardless of how bright or clever you believe yourself to be, verbally engaging an attacking vampire only works in your opponent's favor.

Do Not Listen—As important as it is to avoid speaking directly to your undead opponent, disregarding any communication coming from the vampire during combat is just as critical. A vampire will often attempt a psychological attack should the tide of battle begin to turn. Hence, if a vampire tries to coerce you into conversation, it is likely that it feels in jeopardy. However, the psychological onslaught from the creature can be as powerful as its bodily assault. A vampire will compliment, cajole, insult, and manipulate you in order to draw you into a verbal joust, and its ability to do so is extraordinarily seductive. You must not pay attention to any of the creature's statements or inquiries, and absolutely do not reveal any personal details to your opponent. This is especially true if your adversary is someone you knew previously in their human existence. There is no doubt that the creature will use this past knowledge to take advantage of the situation. A seemingly inconsequential detail in a human conversation can provide an opening that a vampire can use to psychologically overpower its target without lifting an undead finger.

III. CONDITIONING AND PREPARATION

SPIRITUAL PREPARATION

One of the misconceptions discussed in the opening chapter was the myth that vampires are in any way connected to a spiritual or metaphysical context. It was made emphatically clear that relying on any type of religious artifact in your vampire encounter would be wholly ineffective in combat. Why, then, would any type of spiritual preparation be necessary in a hostile engagement with the undead?

While it is true that symbols, artifacts, and paraphernalia associated with any particular religious belief have no effect on a member of the vampire species, human individuals who have some form of spiritual practice do seem to harness benefits that may aid them in undead combat. Research conducted on persons who practice some type of belief system appears to show that such individuals seem to be in better physical health than their nonpracticing counterparts and tend to avoid behaviors that would be detrimental to their well-being; these physical attributes can play a significant role when it comes to prevailing in an undead attack. Outside of the purely physical benefits, spiritual individuals also seem to be capable of drawing upon an inner strength, based on the belief that a higher power may be on their side in a battle against the undead menace. Whether this belief is accurate or not is insignificant; the placebo effect generated by such a belief is enough to provide an edge to the spiritual combatant.

It is important to note that this spirituality is not tied to any particular religious sect or belief system. Whether it is faith in a formalized religion such as Buddhism, Islam, Christianity, or Hinduism, or in something more secular in nature such as yoga, meditation, or simple quiet contemplation, any level of spirituality can benefit the combatant when the engagement seems at its most futile. The moments you spend participating in any type of spiritual activity may help you in ways you never would have expected, such as fending off a bloodthirsty ghoul snapping at your throat.

COMBAT NUTRITION

A discussion on nutritional habits may seem out of place in a manual on battling the undead, until you realize that care and maintenance of your primary weapon—your body—is of paramount importance if you are to emerge from a vampire engagement with your bloodlines intact. Regardless of how strong or agile you may be, fueling your body improperly will result in subpar performance when you need it most—during combat.

On the conventional battlefield, soldiers need not put as much individual thought into what they put into their bodies. Their diets are largely regimented by what is provided to them by their commanding units. As a civilian, however, you are left on your own, and have the luxury of making personal nutritional choices, good or bad. It is not uncommon to see professional warriors returning to civilian life and immediately gaining a significant amount of weight once the military regimen, dietary restriction, and stress of combat has been removed from their day-to-day existence. This is not necessarily a bad thing. However, when eating habits begin to degrade battle readiness, it should become a cause for concern. Hopefully the recommendations that follow can provide a general path to living a lifestyle that prepares you not only for better overall health, but to effectively battle the undead.

Let us be clear: The following suggestions are not for your average citizen looking to lose a few pounds or drop a dress size or two (while these may indeed be ancillary benefits of these recommendations). These nutritional principles are meant to maximize your function as a warrior confronting a stronger, undead opponent, and the goals of these recommendations serve three straightforward purposes:

- Provide a steady source of energy
- Improve your physical competencies
- Enhance your combat readiness

What is the optimal nutritional mix for combat, particularly against a bloodsucking ghoul? In the same way you must conduct a thorough self-assessment of your body type and tailor your conditioning to suit your physique, the same objective assessment must be made regarding your eating regimen. Rather than provide complicated lists of specific foods that should and should not be consumed, we believe it is much more beneficial to pattern your dietary habits around a set of broader concepts that you can apply to your lifestyle as a warrior against the undead. Using these concepts as your guideposts, you are not constantly weighing, measuring, and monitoring your food intake, but are still benefiting from a healthy nutritional regimen that can support the energy required to battle the undead in all its forms. Any individual, regardless of build and combatant type, can benefit from applying even just one of the following concepts:

Stoke Your Furnace—Each year, millions of people begin a diet for various reasons. Most of them fail. The word "diet" in itself carries with it negative connotations—deprivation, sacrifice, denial—which is the reason a majority of people who follow any type of forced consumption ritual are doomed to failure. Rather, you should think of your nutritional intake as an integral part of your preparation—one that either maximizes your combat capabilities or hinders them.

Imagine yourself as a machine; the food you consume fuels the engine, enabling you to perform at your peak in every type of physical encounter. Although easy to preach, this practice may be difficult for many to apply, as food serves as much as a source of pleasure as a nutritional resource. The discipline to do what is best for your body will depend on your current vulnerability to vampire attack and your desire to survive. Before putting any morsel of food into your mouth, think to yourself, "Does eating this make me a better warrior?"

Go Natural—Eating foods that are closest to their unprocessed, unadulterated state is the best strategy for keeping your body running at top performance. Fruits, vegetables, nuts, and meats free from pesticides, hormones, and additives are the optimal choices for daily consumption. Avoid processed and fast foods like the plague—they provide little nutritional value, particularly compared to their natural counterparts, and can actually impede your effectiveness in combat by supplying an inferior source of fuel for your body.

Eat in Color—The color white has traditionally represented the good, the wholesome, the pure. It is ironic that when it comes to food, the reality is often the exact opposite. White flour, white potatoes, white sugar, white rice: these items are considered refined carbohydrates, and processed by the body rapidly, causing spikes in insulin levels and undesired fat gain. In contrast, often the most healthful items are those vibrant in color: leafy greens, vegetables, and fruits. Healthier alternatives exist for all refined carbohydrate items in every case: whole grains, yams, and brown rice—carbohydrates that provide better nutritional value and more sustained energy to keep you in the fight.

Power through Protein—As a combatant-in-training, you will no doubt be expending a great deal of energy, particularly if you follow any of the fitness recommendations provided in this text. As you strain your body through intense physical activity, the muscle fibers break down, which the body then repairs, making them stronger to handle future bouts of exertion. In order to continue to build quality muscle and recover from strenuous conditioning, it is crucial to ingest proper amounts of protein. While most ordinary civilians probably consume adequate amounts for their somewhat sedentary lifestyle, you are no ordinary civilian. This is not to say that it is necessary to devour a porterhouse steak several times a day, but plan to consume a moderate quantity of protein the approximate size of your palm at every meal, be it meat, fish, poultry, or vegetable sources.

Break the Rules—One day every week, you are to disregard every recommendation previously mentioned. You can eat what you want, when you want it, from the minute you wake until you lay your body down to rest for the night. No food is off-limits, just for this one day. Not only is this "off" day beneficial; it is essential to your success the remainder of the week. The primary reason why many diets are unsuccessful is because they do not account for the fact that we are human. Unlike our undead opponents, we crave things other than blood. Without a dietary release valve to look forward to one day out of the week, we are destined to fail at some point. If you have followed all the previous nutritional concepts throughout the week, allow yourself the luxury to consume anything you wish on this day, and resume as normal afterward. You will soon find that your cravings can be satiated without needing to gorge unceasingly, and you will actually look forward to getting back to a healthy, combatant-minded lifestyle the following day.

COMBAT REPORT:
CHERIE LOUISSANT

Restaurateur
New Orleans, Louisiana

Cherie Louissant, known as "Mama Cherie" to her friends and customers, is a third-generation restaurant owner in New Orleans. Cherie's Place has been serving patrons in the Ninth Ward for more than thirty years. Like many businesses in the region, Louissant's establishment was devastated by Hurricane Katrina. Unlike many business owners, Louissant returned to the area and rebuilt her restaurant just as it was before the storm.

The room is filled with patrons of all kinds on the night I visit—businessmen, tourists, and locals alike sit and feast upon her authentic Creole dishes. I'm told by the manager that the restaurant was rebuilt exactly as it looked before the hurricane, with one exception. He points to the walls, which show the stain of the high-water mark where the flood waters reached. "Cherie wanted to rebuild, but not forget."

The manager guides me through the crowded main room and into the back of the house, where Mama Cherie is expediting the orders and inspecting the dishes coming out, otherwise known as "the pass." I'm told that up until a few years ago, Louissant was still cooking meals until arthritis finally got the best of her hands. She is a slight, frail-looking woman, but her grip is astonishingly strong when she shakes my hand, the result of decades spent laboring in her kitchen. She guides me to the chef's table: a unique attribute in a casual dining spot such as Cherie's Place. Traditionally found only in upscale restaurants, part dining experience, part theater, the chef's table is an attraction in the kitchen where diners can watch the cooks prepare the meals as they eat. A mammoth bowl of Cherie's famous jambalaya is placed in front of me, and I eat while watching Louissant move lightly back and forth from dish to dish, meticulously scrutinizing it for service. My bowl is empty moments later. Cherie joins me at the table while her staff continues to work. A curtain is drawn around the table to provide us some privacy and silence from the din of the kitchen.

Cherie Louissant: Looks like you enjoyed my jambalaya.

Vampire Combat Manual: The best I've ever had.

CL: That's sweet of you, dear. I'm just glad I'm able to do what I can for these folks. It was touch and go for a while after the storm, you know. Everybody said they were going to come back, that they wouldn't let Mother Nature drive them out, but it was tougher going than we thought. I don't blame those who left though; things weren't so pleasant here for a long time. Still aren't for some, but we're doing the best we can with what we got.

VCM: I'm sure that was very difficult for you, as a lifelong resident.

CL: I remember that day like it was yesterday. The rain itself wasn't so bad at all, just a bit of water and wind; we all seen that before. After she had passed, it looked like we were going to be just fine. I remember seeing people dancing and singing on Bourbon Street. Then, well, the levees gave way, and things got real difficult. I remember lots of people in other parts of the country kept asking, "Why did you stay? Why didn't you leave when you had the chance?" There's something that folks not from here don't really understand. This city can be a rough place. The only thing some people got here is their homes. If you're scared or uneasy, the one thing you can count on is the security of your own house. That's why people stayed; they know that when it's frightening outside, they can be safe inside. This time that wasn't the case.

VCM: This city has a long history with the occult, doesn't it?

CL: Oh sure, that comes from the original groups who settled here. Louisiana's got a mess of influences—European from the French and Spanish, Caribbean from the Haitian exiles, and African, of course, from the slave trade. Each of those groups has their own superstitions and hoodoo-voodoo nonsense. Back in the day that may have been more popular, but now it's just a bunch of fairytales to sell books and movies and get the tourists coming back. What a funny question. Why do you ask?

VCM: There's something I'd like to show you.

CL: What is it, child?

I open my bag and remove the empty blood packet used by Jason Richter during our meeting. I traced the packaging through various drop shipments across the country, back into the port of New Orleans. After deciphering scores of shipping manifests, many of them falsified, I tracked the shipments to a warehouse under the name of Roosevelt Bulger, a relative of Louissant who has been dead for 20 years. She takes the packet from my hands and manipulates it for several minutes between her knotted fingers. Finally, she looks up at me. The warmth in her eyes is gone.

CL: Follow me.

Before I can respond, she shifts the dining table slightly to the left and back, which triggers a false wall behind her. Louissant pushes against the wall, opening it farther, and disappears into the darkness. I follow her into the passageway. We walk for what feels like miles, deep into a twisting maze of corridors and passageways, hewn from the earth and supported by ancient wooden beams.

We finally arrive at what appears to be a storage and assembly area. Deep beneath the earth's surface, the room is naturally frigid. Hundreds of full packets like the empty container in my possession line the walls. A single worker is busy packing them into insulated crates. When he notices my presence, he ceases his work and stares at me until Louissant takes me by the hand and gives him a reassuring look. We proceed past the storage facility into a much larger room lined with the same seating arrangements used in the restaurant. Individuals are seated at several of the tables. Even in the dim light of the room, it is clear that they are not human. Many of them appear to have facial deformities indicating that they are of the Grotesque vampire caste. They stop feeding from the packets and stiffen at my presence until Louissant again provides a calming glance. She pauses for a moment, allowing me to look around but never releasing my hand. We return back the way we came. As we walk through the winding passageways, Louissant begins to speak again.

CL: When I was a child, my mawmaw told me a story about her gramma, my great-great-grandma. She was a plantation slave. One night, she managed to escape with her baby boy, my great-grandpa. She ran all night long with a crying child in her arms. With nowhere to go and a cold, hungry baby to care for, she took a chance and knocked on the door of a random home. Now, most white folks back then would have done one thing if she rang their bell—taken her back to the plantation where she probably would have been whipped within an inch of her life, maybe her baby too. But the man who opened that door to her didn't. He didn't know them. He didn't owe them nothin'. But he knew what would happen if he brought them back. He risked his life to help her and her boy. He got them to the Railroad, and they were eventually free. My granny always used that story to say, "When someone's in trouble and asking for help, you don't look at who they are. You look at what they need."

Katrina took away a lot from this city. Everybody was hurting bad. *Everybody.* And when everybody is hurting, you have to help take away that pain. That's what I'm doing back there—taking away the pain. It's not just for them, you see; it's also for us. Lots of people left the city and didn't come back. People who also used to help. What do you think happens to the folks you saw down there if I don't help them? They get hungry. They get desperate. And when they get desperate, bad things will happen. If we don't do something to help, well, then the city will really be lost.

We arrive back at the passageway entrance at the chef's table. The curtain is still drawn, the kitchen still buzzes with activity, and my empty bowl still sits on the table.

CL: You know that dish, jambalaya, it ain't supposed to work. When the Spanish first came here, they tried to make paella, but they didn't have all the right ingredients, so they started to change the dish. Meat, chicken, seafood, sausage, all thrown together with rice. The mess of ingredients and flavors isn't supposed to work, and if you make it wrong, it doesn't; but when you get it right, the dish works beautifully. The reason's because it's balanced. Every ingredient, every seasoning, works in harmony with another. New Orleans is like jambalaya. We got a mess of different kinds down here. So many kinds that most people looking at it from the outside would think we'd be at each other's throats day and night. Through the years, we've been able to make it work. That perfect combination was thrown off by Mother Nature. If we aren't able to find that balance again and get it back to how it was, I'm scared for what's going to come of this place.

Louissant takes my hand and grips it firmly, as if to ensure my full attention. The softness returns to her eyes.

CL: I know what you're trying to do, child. I know you think you're doing good. But be careful. Sometimes it's best to let things simmer than to stir up the pot.

IV.

WEAPONS

Weapons are an important factor in war, but not the decisive one; it is man and not materials that counts.

—MAO TSE-TUNG

The vampire's transformative process is a supremely intelligent one; it provides the host with all the tools required for hunting human prey while simultaneously insulating it from the dangers of most common weaponry, even in today's technologically advanced age. What makes a vampire engagement so hazardous for the human population is not only the creature's superior physical attributes, but also the dearth of weapons that can be used successfully against it in battle. In vampire combat, you must pay close attention to the armaments chosen to aid in your defense; only a select few will be truly effective in neutralizing your undead attacker.

Before delving into our analysis of what armaments work well against this particular foe, let us begin by reviewing which tools are largely *ineffective* in vampire combat. Heed these cautions, and never make the mistake of assuming a weapon that works against a human opponent will also work against a creature with a humanoid appearance such as the vampire.

Firearms—Rifles, pistols, machine guns; firepower is often seen as the great equalizer in a battle between two mismatched adversaries, and is the weapon of choice throughout the world. In undead combat, shooting a vampire with a firearm is as effective as throwing the weapon itself. The regenerative factors possessed by the creature will heal a majority of wounds inflicted by most firearms before they cause any permanent damage, even those weapons whose projectile size causes significant trauma in human opponents. While the use of silver in bullets can effectively

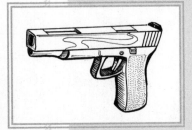

cause damage in the same fashion as the element itself, it is impractical for all but the wealthiest of individuals to have custom-made silver-jacketed ammunition. There are some exceptions regarding the inadequacy of firearms in vampire combat, and it is also important to note that while firearms are ineffective against the vampire itself, they can be used against any of the creature's human sympathizers.

Bludgeons—Just as a vampire's healing ability prevents any permanent damage from firearms, bludgeoning implements are mostly ineffective in undead neutralization. Striking a vampire with a cudgel-like object such as a club, mace, or staff will serve only to enrage it further while causing no significant bodily harm. The only exception to this rule is if the blow is so powerful that it rends the head of the creature completely from its spine, a feat that most human combatants are unable to accomplish. The only purpose bludgeons serve in vampire combat is to provide a momentary distraction to your opponent before you launch a more substantial attack.

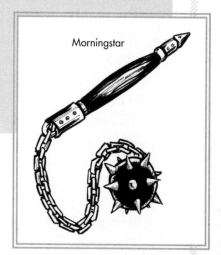

Morningstar

Exotic Weapons—Due to the popularity of martial arts and fantasy films, many individuals believe that exotic weaponry such as shuriken (throwing stars),

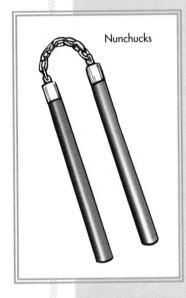

Nunchucks

nunchaku (nunchucks), and kama (sickle) are viable options for vampire combat. What better way to dismantle an opponent than with the unique and seemingly effective weapons seen on the big screen? Although there is a clear attraction factor to using these unusual arms in combat, do not allow yourself to be lulled into this fantasy. There are two very important reasons why esoteric weapons are poor choices in vampire combat.

First, consider that regardless of the weapon, you are still limited by the constraints of your opponent's vulnerabilities. Whether it is done with a bowie knife, a sickle, or a Shaolin monk's spade, a slashing laceration wound on a vampire will heal, often within seconds of the initial strike. The second and more important detail to consider is your personal level of skill with the weapon. While some armaments are easily mastered, exotic tools such as those previously mentioned take years of dedicated practice to gain just an average level of proficiency. While there are certainly a handful of individuals who could use these devices to neutralize an opponent, would you consider yourself one of them? If not, choose a more standard armament in your battle against the undead.

BALLISTIC/ LONG-RANGE WEAPONS

Having covered weapons that are poor choices in vampire combat, let us turn our attention to armaments that can turn the tide in your favor during an undead encounter. Ballistic or long-range weapons are defined as those that fire some type of projectile at your opponent. Weapons within this class are often comprised mostly of firearms, which as we now know are generally not effective against the vampire species. There are, however, a limited number of ballistic weapon types that could be added to your arsenal, provided you are fully aware of their limitations.

Compound Bow

RANGE: **10–20 METERS**
FIRE RATE: **SLOW**
SKILL LEVEL: **EXTREMELY HIGH**

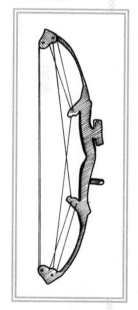

Description: The bow and arrow is one of the most primitive and effective of all long-range projectile weapons. Used throughout history both for hunting and combat purposes, this weapon can be extremely effective in the hands of a skilled archer. The compound bow improves on the original design by incorporating a set of pulley wheels, known as cams, on both ends of the weapon. This system of cams and levers creates a much easier draw on the bowstring and reduces the strength required to pull back and fire the arrow accurately.

Any weapon that enables you to execute a terminating blow while maintaining a safe distance from your

IV. WEAPONS

target is attractive from a combat perspective. In a vampire engagement, the compound bow can be used to target the heart of your opponent at a longer range, providing a way to neutralize your target without requiring you to engage it up close. This weapon system can also be utilized to deliver a finishing blow once a creature has been properly secured, averting the need to utilize a more intimate and unpleasant means of disposal, such as staking or decapitation.

The compound bow also has some drawbacks in vampire combat that should be properly noted. The greatest liability to using a bow during an undead encounter is the skill level required to deliver an accurate strike at long range. In a historical combat setting, an arrow piercing any part of the human body can achieve incapacitating damage. In combat with the undead, the archer must strike an area the approximate size of a fist on a moving target—a difficult feat for even the most skilled bowman. Therefore, the range of this weapon against an undead attacker is markedly less than what it would be in a regular combat setting. Should you miss your target with the first strike, it is unlikely that you will have a second opportunity, as your opponent will likely either escape or rapidly close the distance. The final liability to note is that most arrows constructed today are made from synthetic materials, not the historically wooden shafts originally used for this weapon. Any non-wood-based arrow will not cause the desired reaction even if your strike penetrates the vampire heart.

Crossbow

RANGE: **15 METERS**
FIRE RATE: **SLOW**
SKILL LEVEL: **HIGH**

Description: An advancement in weaponry so formidable for its time that it is rumored Pope Innocent II banned its use in 1139, the crossbow incorporates the shape and trigger mechanism of a firearm with the projectile of the arrow bolt. The greatest benefit of the crossbow over the conventional bow is the minimal amount

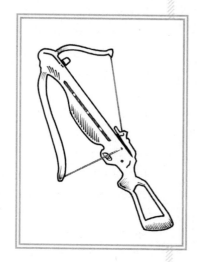

of skill required to use the weapon. Whereas the bow requires extensive training, strength, and skill to accurately strike a target with any degree of consistency, the crossbow enables any man, woman, or child able to point and fire the weapon to use it effectively. This weapon is also a solid alternative for those with physical disabilities that make use of a regular bow awkward.

Similar to its older counterpart, the crossbow can be effective in vampire combat provided you account for its limitations. The construction of this weapon enables you to maintain accuracy even as the drawstring is retracted and ready to fire. A combatant using a crossbow is also able to sustain the weapon in a drawn and ready state for an extended amount of time prior to firing, unlike a normal bow. The best use of this weapon is to fire the bolt into the heart of your undead assailant, neutralizing it from a distance. Although the trajectory of the weapon allows you to keep a distance from your opponent when firing, the range is not as great as the standard bow.

IV. WEAPONS

The liabilities of the crossbow in vampire combat are virtually identical to those of the regular bow. You'll note that the ranges provided for both of these bowstring armaments may seem much shorter than the actual range a competent archer is able to achieve with either weapon. The reasoning for this is simple. In vampire combat, it is unlikely that you will be able to neutralize a vampire from a long distance, unless your target is completely stationary and oblivious to your attack, and you are an Olympic-caliber marksman. Realistically, the range for either the bow or the crossbow in an undead engagement is quite short. Due to these significant shortcomings, these two projectile weapons are recommended only for special circumstances where you can ensure your strike will hit its mark and not necessitate a follow-up attack.

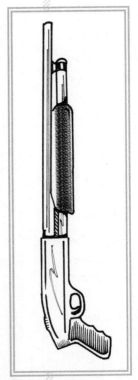

Shotgun

RANGE: **1–5 METERS**
FIRE RATE: **MEDIUM**
SKILL LEVEL: **MEDIUM**

Description: Although most firearms are ineffective when confronting a vampiric attacker due to its accelerated healing factor, there is one exception to this guideline: the shotgun. A weapon that is common in sporting, hunting, and the personal safety arena, shotguns fire shells that contain either round pellets known as shot or solid projectiles called slugs. This firearm is popular for home defense due to its effectiveness in close quarters and the lack of aiming precision required, resulting from the spray pattern generated by the shot projectiles.

Decapitation and dismemberment are possible tactics in vampire combat, and the shotgun is one of the few firearms that has the ability to accomplish either at close range. A well-placed blast has the potential to sever limbs and, if targeted properly, remove the head altogether. The discharge from this weapon also has the capability to knock your opponent backward a short distance, enabling you to either escape or follow up with an additional attack. It is for these reasons that the shotgun is one of the few firearms that has true promise in a vampire engagement.

Due to the popularity of the shotgun as a "game-changing" weapon with extreme stopping power, it is important to convey the fact that the shotgun's performance in undead combat should not be misjudged. Many overconfident combatants have relied on the reputation of this weapon only to find themselves in dire straits once its limitations reveal themselves against an attacking succubus. In order to perform the type of shots that are capable of severing limbs, the combatant must be in fairly close proximity to the target. Too great a distance, and the dispersal pattern of the shot will wound rather than amputate the target. Thanks to the vampire's healing ability, minor shot wounds will mend themselves much like other types of superficial trauma. Although precise aim is not required with this weapon, it does take a moderate amount of skill to wield the shotgun effectively. Should this be one of your primary ballistic weapons, practice with it extensively, mimicking its use in an undead situation by aiming at specific areas such as the appendages and head. The last situation in which you want to discover how difficult it is to blow the limb clean off an attacking vampire is when the creature is seconds away from clutching your throat.

Some may argue that certain high-caliber firearms are equally capable of the requisite damage that can be performed by the shotgun. This is absolutely true. However, rifles and handguns of this type are often difficult to obtain and challenging to wield for the everyday citizen with minimal firearms training. Remember also that with the shotgun, the shot dispersal means that pinpoint accuracy is not as crucial; not so with a single bullet shot from a high-powered firearm.

Fire
RANGE: **3.3–6.6 METERS**
FIRE RATE: **SLOW**
SKILL LEVEL: **LOW**

Description: Although difficult to control and potentially devastating to both attacker and defender, fire can be used against the undead as a neutralizing weapon, provided it is wielded with extreme care. A vampire, fully immolated and immersed in flames, will eventually expire, its healing mechanisms unable to keep up with the pronounced and continuous cellular damage caused by the blaze. However, most vampires will not allow themselves to succumb to this fate so easily, and will do everything in their power to extinguish themselves once alight.

The optimal use of fire in vampire combat is to utilize the

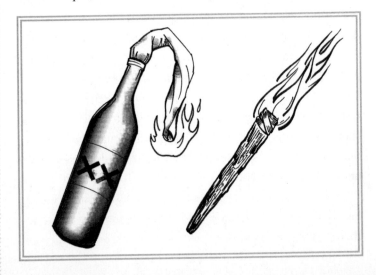

element to set the attacker alight while simultaneously confining your opponent within a specific area where it is unable to escape and douse the flames. The best time to use this unruly weapon is when you are attacking the vampire at its resting grounds, preferably during daylight hours. Utilizing fire in the vampire abode has the added benefit of destroying the creature's place of rest as well as the being itself. Caution must be used in such a setting, however, as vampires often take up residence in locations where innocent humans also reside; setting fire to a nest located in a public complex is also liable to engulf the entire structure. Should you find yourself in such a setting, be prepared to manage the blaze and extinguish the flames the moment you can confirm that your adversary has been terminated. Fire can turn from ally to adversary in a heartbeat; responsibility with this weapon is advised.

MELEE WEAPONS

At melee range, defined specifically in vampire combat as a distance of two to four feet between opponents, you are severely hampered in your ability to terminate your opponent due to its limited vulnerabilities. At this distance, one of the most effective weapons at your disposal is a bladed implement. When it comes to vampire combat, all edged weapons are not created equal. The type of blade available should dictate your method of attack. The converse also holds true; should you find yourself adept at a particular type of offensive technique, ensure that you have a weapon at the ready that is better suited to your combat style.

Given the wide variety of edged weapons available, we have classified the various types of bladed armaments into three distinct categories:

Heavy Blades—Weapons within this class are defined by their wide, substantial striking faces, and include armaments such as battle-axes and halberds, and improvised weapons such as fire axes and camp hatchets. Heavy blades are most appropriately used for a decapitation strike, where their weighted ends can deliver a forceful blow to the neck region of your opponent, separating the vampire head from its torso in a powerful swipe.

The greatest liability of this edged-weapon class, and the reason why dismembering attacks are not encouraged with these armaments without extensive training, is the narrow striking surface area of the blade, which is much shorter than other types of edged weapons. The lethal edge of a heavy-bladed weapon is concentrated in a small region at the very end of the armament's handle, and, as such, requires a greater amount of strength, timing, and skill to deliver an accurate blow. A prepared vampire can easily dodge a heavy oncoming strike, particularly if the blow is directed toward a smaller, more mobile area such as the creature's forearm or the kneecap. Users of heavy blades are also more prone to losing their balance given the greater heft of the weapon. Formal instruction with this class of blade is encouraged, particularly if it is your primary vampire combat weapon.

Long Blades—Edged weapons in the long blade class include all sword types, such as broadswords, katanas, and claymores. Of our three blade classes, this one is the most adaptable, as it is capable of both a decapitation strike and a dismembering blow. The longer edge of the blade makes it much easier to attack various areas without as much concern for missing your target.

The long blade, however, is not without its liabilities, the most significant of which is its conspicuous nature and lack of concealability. Most law enforcement organizations frown upon citizens carrying a long sword on their person. While the same can be said for a heavy-bladed weapon, axes have a valid functional use for many professions and are more prevalent within our society. The same cannot be said for a samurai sword. Like heavy blades, armaments in this class should be wielded by a trained hand for maximum effectiveness.

Melee Blades—Bladed arms in this class comprise weapons with shorter edges, roughly twelve to twenty inches in length, and include such weapons as the machete, barong, and kukri blade. Lighter, faster, and more concealable than the other classes, short blades are also the most affordable of the three classes of edged weapons. Given their length, however,

IV. WEAPONS

decapitation strikes are not recommended with this blade class.

While it is clearly possible to execute a decapitating maneuver with a melee blade, it may take several blows to do so. Recall your opponent's extraordinary healing ability. When using a bladed weapon, you are essentially playing a game of "beat the clock" against the vampire's restorative capabilities. A minor flesh wound created by a short-bladed armament will heal rapidly, provided the weapon is not laced with silver. Your best option with a melee blade weapon is a maiming blow to the limb extremities on the vampire's torso, such as the forearms, wrists, and ankles. A powerful blow to one of these narrow regions, even with a blade of this length, has the ability to sever the appendage of your attacker. Although such a blow won't be terminal to the creature, it will more than likely cause your attacker to cease its assault and retreat in order to heal its wounds.

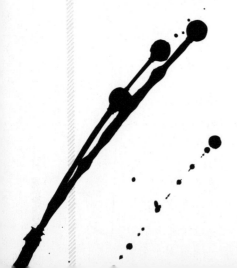

CLOSE-QUARTERS WEAPONS

Close-quarters combat is the most treacherous range to engage any opponent, be they living or undead. Unfortunately, it is also the most common range at which vampire combat occurs. A vampire's ultimate objective in any human engagement is to position itself as close as possible to the target, open a bloodline, and commence its feeding session. In order to successfully defend yourself against a vampire's onslaught and launch a counterattack of your own, you will need to not only be skilled at close-quarters techniques, but also prepared with the appropriate weapon.

Stake
RANGE: <1 FOOT (.3 METERS)
AVAILABILITY: COMMON
SKILL LEVEL: EXTREMELY HIGH

While there are a variety of armaments to choose from in vampire combat, the most essential and recognized of all weapons is the simple stake. Nothing more than a sharpened length of wood, this primal and seemingly unimpressive weapon strikes fear into the heart of every vampire, and should be the cornerstone of your combat arsenal and weapons training. As such, we will spend a significant portion of this section articulating the properties, uses, and finer details that make the stake an effective close-combat weapon in a vampire engagement.

The stake is such an ordinary weapon that its subtleties are often lost on the untrained citizen. Although mundane in nature, there are several factors you must consider when preparing your staking weapon for vampire combat.

Material Composition

What is the specific element present within wood that initiates the neutralization process when thrust into the heart of the vampire? That is still unclear. Some have attributed it to the natural resins contained within the cellulose fibers. Others have hypothesized that wood's primary function as a transport system for minerals and nutrients from the earth throughout a plant's vascular system is what triggers the self-detonating reaction in the undead. What has been established is that regardless of the type, structure, or chemistry, all wood will cause the same violent reaction in the undead once the stake has penetrated the creature's heart.

Wood Types—While any type of wood will work in crafting your staking implement, certain types are preferable to others. Different varieties of trees produce wood of varying densities. Should you have the time to select particular materials, construct your stakes from the hardest wood possible. Do not be confused by the terms "softwood" and "hardwood" in your search for materials, as these categories are related more to the plant's scientific classification than the density of the wood itself, with some hardwoods being softer in density than certain softwood varietals.

The following is a list of both woody plants whose structure makes excellent staking material and low-density woods you should avoid if at all possible.

HIGH-DENSITY WOODS

- Walnut
- Teak
- Oak
- Ebony
- Apple
- Maple
- Cocobolo
- Mahogany

LOW-DENSITY WOODS

- Cedar
- Willow
- Aspen
- Redwood
- Basswood
- Yew
- Pine (White/Yellow)
- Spruce

The stakes should be crafted from wood that has already been harvested and seasoned, and not taken directly from living "green" specimens. Using material from a living plant means that your wood will contain a considerable amount of moisture, which can affect its density and resiliency in combat. Should you have only live material at your disposal, an alternative solution is to dry the stakes in the sunlight or over an open flame. The heat will cause the moisture within the wood to evaporate, creating a much sturdier weapon.

Avoid any synthetic or engineered wood products, such as particleboard, plywood, or any laminated timbers during your selection process. These materials are comprised mostly of wood and wood by-products such as sawdust, chips, and wood shavings. While stakes created from such material may work against an attacking vampire, they are generally less sturdy and are prone to breakage compared to lumber harvested directly from trees. During a vampire engagement, not only must you pierce a vampire's heart with your staking

IV. WEAPONS

weapon; you must ensure that your opponent does not destroy the implement before you have an opportunity to use it. Quite possibly the most depressing sight to witness would be your undead opponent splintering your plywood stake with a swat of its fist.

Weapon Dimensions

Just as important as the source materials for creating your staking armament are the physical dimensions of the weapon itself. This may seem like a minor consideration, but such factors can be critical in your ability to successfully employ the weapon in combat without it being too flimsy to impale the heart of your opponent or too unwieldy to complete its intended task.

Determining the dimensions of your stake is a personalized endeavor. What may work for a 110-pound, left-handed female combatant may not be ideal for a 220-pound, right-handed male civilian. Here are some of the factors you should consider when constructing your stake:

Length—The length of the stake is one of the most important decisions a vampire combatant can make when customizing his weapon, and is often miscalculated. The error many combatants often make is crafting a weapon that is much too long for its intended purpose. When it comes to a vampire stake, bigger is not necessarily better. Not only is a longer stake more susceptible to breakage, it may affect your ability to execute a fast, neutralizing blow. The longer the weapon, the less fine control you have over its direction when thrusting it toward your target, resulting in a greater margin of error for your strike. A combatant using a staking weapon must also take into account the direction of attack. Depending on the entry point on the vampire torso, you may require a weapon that is longer or shorter in order to reach its target.

Diameter/Width—The diameter or width of the stake is as important as the overall length of your weapon. Keep in mind that you are executing a gouging attack into your attacker. Unlike a weapon forged from metals, the wooden stake is a relatively fragile implement crafted from natural material that is prone to breakage. Utilize too narrow a width, and your weapon is liable to snap or splinter before it reaches its final target. On the other hand, crafting a stake with too wide a diameter may also be detrimental in combat, with your weapon's path blocked by muscle and bone, its thickness unable to penetrate deeply enough into your undead opponent's body cavity.

Bevel—While the inexperienced vampire combatant may believe that "a sharpened point is a sharpened point," there is actually a great deal of intricacy that goes into honing a weapon's point for a neutralizing thrust. A stake with a long, narrow point may be able to penetrate your opponent more easily, but can also be fragile and liable to fracture before fully entering your adversary. A wider, stubbier point, like that of a chisel, has superb resiliency and hardiness, but may require a greater amount of strength to force into the vampire's chest cavity. It may be the case that you do not have the luxury of determining the optimal angle for your sharpened stake. Should you have the time, however, to craft your own weapon, be sure to whittle a point that is neither too narrow nor too wide, so that your armament can be used for the widest range of staking attacks.

Optimal Stake Design

Given all the possibilities for variation and customization, is there one universal design that is optimal for most vampire encounters? Based on general anatomy, anecdotal evidence from vampire engagements, and analysis conducted by IUCS researchers, the following design parameters seem to work well for the majority of vampire encounters.

OPTIMAL STAKING DIMENSIONS:

- **Length**—12–18" long. A stake of this length offers a comfortable, full-handed grip while still allowing enough of the weapon to extend past the hand, enter the target, and deliver a neutralizing strike from any direction.

- **Width**—1–1.5" in diameter. A stake with an inch-wide diameter allows the combatant to grip the weapon solidly with minimal risk of slipping from his grasp, as well as providing enough mass to withstand several stabbing blows into the vampire torso without fear of breakage.

- **Bevel**—15 degrees. A sharpened stake crafted with a fifteen-degree hypotenuse bevel creates a tip that is both narrow enough to slip swiftly into an opponent and sturdy enough to withstand damage.

- **Detail**—Double-ended attack points. Perhaps the most important detail in crafting your staking weapon, sharpening both ends of the weapon provides the versatility to allow you to take hold of the weapon at a moment's notice and lash out without fear of having seized it from the wrong end.

While these parameters are recommendations based on extensive professional research, they should not circumvent any personal preferences you may have based on your individual traits and combat style. Crafting a vampire stake is a personal undertaking, as is the engagement during which the weapon will be deployed; it is of utmost importance that you design your weapon to your specific requirements.

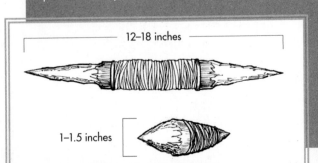

12–18 inches

1–1.5 inches

Retention Methods

Equally as important as the physical characteristics of your staking weapon is the manner in which you affix it to your body. Do not make this decision lightly. What may seem like an afterthought can make the difference between survival and exsanguination. Many a combatant has met a tragic end while fumbling about in an attempt to draw his weapon at the critical moment during a vampire attack.

There are ten possible locations on the human body to carry your staking weapon. Each of these positions is unique and equally effective, offering its own set of advantages and drawbacks, depending on the type of defense and attack methods you employ against an assaulting ghoul.

Back Mount—Securing staking weapons across the upper back is a unique method of retention in anticipation of a vampire attack. Strapped across the same side as the dominant staking hand or along both the left and right trapezius muscles of the back, storing weapons in the back mount is particularly effective when using a downward stabbing motion, holding the  weapon in what is known as the "ice-pick grip." The disadvantage of using this retention method is that it requires a specialized accessory in order to strap the stakes across the back. The weapon may also be difficult to retrieve if an outergarment is worn to cover the stakes, such as a jacket or overcoat. Stakes in the back mount may be hard to access should the

IV. WEAPONS

vampire throw the victim to the ground and onto his back during the course of an attack, with the victim's own weight pinning the weapons underneath.

Waist Mount—A common carrying method used for bladed weapons, tucking a stake into the waist belt is a practical and accessible manner of retaining weapons without the need of any special equipment. The weapon can be stored either in front or on the side of the pelvis or in the small of the back using a belt or a scabbard to secure the weapon in place. In this least conspicuous of all the carry methods, stakes can be easily obscured from public view by covering them with an article of clothing, but still readily available with a draw of the hand. With practice, a waist-mounted stake can be drawn with speed much like that of a firearm or knife. The primary disadvantage to using the waist-mount carry method is comfort. Carrying on normal, everyday activities with a wooden stake tucked into the belt can be an uncomfortable practice.

Leg Mount—There are two options when storing your staking weapon on the lower half of the body: the "drop leg" and "calf cradle" mounts. The drop leg mount retains the weapon along the outside of the thigh at approximately wrist level, similar to how military and law enforcement personnel often carry a drop-holstered sidearm. The drop leg method is a convenient way to retain the stake and have it available at a moment's notice, as the weapon lies just a few inches away from a resting hand. In the calf cradle mount,

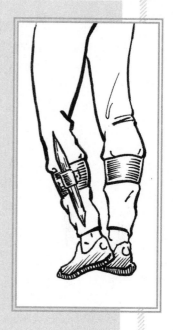

the stake will be strapped to the side of the calf muscle, alongside the outer fibula bone. Those who commonly wear cowboy or calf-length boots tend to prefer this mount, as the weapon can be easily stored on the boot material itself, much like a hideaway knife or firearm holster. The greatest disadvantage of mounting stakes to the lower body is their prominent nature. Positioned in this method outside of clothing on the lower body, the weapons are exposed for all the world to see, including the vampire. If a weapon in the calf cradle mount is concealed by trouser or skirt fabric, immediate accessibility to the weapon is obstructed, and an extra step is required to hike up the clothing material before drawing the weapon.

Arm Mount—Similar to the leg mounting methods, there are two areas on the arms where staking weapons can be stored: either biceps mount or forearm mount. Due to the proximity to grasping hands, using arm-mounted stakes can be very logical, especially when draw speed is of the essence. Weapon storage along the length of the forearm is a method that has been used throughout history to retain bladed implements where speed and clandestine carry were high priorities. During World War I, the Office of Strategic Services, the precursor to the Central Intelligence Agency, devised a "hideout" blade that could be affixed to the forearm and drawn when its use was critical to the agent's survival.

Also similar to the leg mount, the greatest disadvantage in housing weapons along the arms is that, unless shielded by clothing, it is blatantly obvious that you are prepared for a vampire attack. This is less of a concern when traveling in a high-risk environment, but can be difficult if a low profile is desired among the human populace. Additionally, there is a risk of having the weapon snatched from the arm mounting by an attacking vampire, and tossed away before it mounts its own attack.

Optimal Retention Methods

With the wide variety of places on the body to store your staking weapon, is there an optimal location in which to do so? The answer largely depends on your day-to-day situation and the type of staking method preferred during combat. Those who prefer to use an ice-pick grip and strike with a downward stabbing motion into the target will probably prefer the back mount, while those who need to blend into society will probably choose a waist mount option. The fact is that most experienced vampire combatants do not rely on a single carrying method for all their stakes. Often they will utilize at least two, if not more, places to house a close combat weapon, in case one of the locations is compromised and to allow for a variety of attack alternatives.

Just as you should customize the design characteristics of your staking armament, you must also customize your weapon retention method. This will be dictated not only by your level of comfort and need for concealment, but also your ability to access the weapon with minimal interference should a vampire engagement occur unexpectedly.

Gripping Methods

A wooden stake is truly a marvel when it comes to vampire combat. Cheap, ubiquitous, and effective, this rudimentary weapon can neutralize a hostile succubus quickly and efficiently, provided you are fully trained in its use. The first element of this training is using the proper grip. Like many other details in vampire combat, the subtleties of gripping your staking weapon are often lost on the general public. In fact, the manner in which you clasp your hand around this weapon will largely dictate the method by which you can effectively strike the vampire heart. Likewise, should you be intent on attacking your target from a specific direction, the proper grip can make the difference between a terminating blow and a mere flesh wound. Study the various grips carefully, keeping in mind the differences in each and how it will affect the type of blow you deliver to your attacker.

Hammer Grip—Place the stake in your palm with the tip facing upward, and grip it as you would hold a regular hammer: fingers curled around the dowel and thumb folded over the top of the hand. This grip is preferred by a majority of vampire combatants due to its familiarity and comfort, and is best used when targeted at your undead adversary's heart with an upward strike, driving from underneath the rib cage toward the heart or through the center of the chest if the vampire is bent forward.

Ice-Pick Grip—Grip the weapon with the tip facing downward and your hand positioned toward the end of the stake. Blows executed with a stake positioned in this grip are very powerful, due to the force of gravity and the momentum generated from your hand plunging in a downward motion into your opponent with the might of your upper body behind your strike. The ice-pick grip can be used when targeting your opponent's heart from the rear, or when the creature is pinned to the floor, where you can drive the weapon forcefully through the center of its chest.

Reinforced Ice-Pick Grip—Grip the stake as you would in the standard ice-pick grip, and clasp your opposite palm over the top of your weapon hand. Reinforcing your grip with both hands offers better security and retention, and can help prevent the stake from being knocked from your single hand, as well as providing additional power to the strike by using the strength in both arms simultaneously to drive the weapon into your attacker. Such power may be necessary for the ectocombatant during an undead engagement, particularly when executing direct strikes that must penetrate through layers of musculature and bone.

Saber Grip—This is a grip that can be used for a stake, but is also an effective way to hold an edged weapon in order to provide additional cutting pressure on the blade. Grip your weapon as you would in the hammer grip, but place your thumb along the ridge of the weapon as opposed to folded over the hand. Placement of the thumb in this manner allows for slightly better control, as you can direct the tip of the weapon precisely in the direction you would like to strike, using your thumb as the guide. This precision comes at the slight sacrifice of security, considering you no longer have as tight a grasp as you would using the hammer grip.

SECONDARY WEAPONS

In the realm of vampire combat, there are a number of tools that we define as "secondary weapons"—items that, although useful, do not have the ability to neutralize an attacker vampire by themselves. These are armaments that you will utilize to complement your primary arsenal in your engagement with the undead. Do not, however, confuse "secondary" with "second-class." On the contrary, secondary weapons play a critical part against the undead, and have the ability to save your life should you find yourself in an unfortunate predicament with a rampaging ghoul. The distinction is used merely to distinguish their capabilities from your primary, neutralizing weapons so that no confusion exists as to their inherent use and advantages against the vampire species.

Knives/Edged Tools

In human hand-to-hand combat, a knife can alter the nature of combat between two equally matched foes, and can become an equalizing tool against mismatched adversaries. Given the requirement that a wooden implement be used against the vampire heart and the fact that most knife wounds will heal rapidly on the vampire torso, a common question posed is whether the everyday blade has any place in vampire combat.

Compact edged weapons do have a place in your vampire arsenal, but not in a regular combat role. Rather than an implement to inflict pain, the knife in vampire combat is used for a much more mundane, yet necessary, purpose: to craft your staking implements. Once you have chosen an appropriate segment of wood, it will be necessary to whittle its blunt shape until a sharpened point remains. This explicit task requires a cutting implement appropriate for this type of duty.

The most common mistake made by novice combatants is to select an oversized, unwieldy blade. Although such a knife may be effective in intimidating a human opponent, an undead attacker will not give it a moment's thought. Additionally, if your purpose is to shave away wood, a long, massive blade is not the optimal choice. Beyond the simple fact that it is nearly impossible to conceal, a larger blade makes finer control over the tool more difficult. Some may argue that a larger blade can assist with chopping large pieces of wood into appropriate lengths, but it is much more practical to use a tool more appropriate for this task, such as an axe, hatchet, or machete. The reason that most whittling knives are smaller, with a blade less than six inches long and devoid of serrations, is to provide more control over the blade during the whittling process. Do not be tempted by edged weapons depicted in the realm of entertainment; in the actual world of vampire combat, application is more important than size.

Garlic

As we described in the section on vulnerabilities, garlic is one of the few naturally grown substances that produces an extreme adverse reaction in the undead species. Inexpensive and readily available, garlic can be incorporated into your vampire arsenal in a variety of ways and can be a powerful ally

in your battle against a bloodthirsty ghoul. While it is unlikely that the cloves of the plant can be leveraged to completely eliminate your opponent, garlic can be used as a strong deterrent against an attacking vampire, provided it is used properly.

In addition to being cheap and plentiful, garlic has the advantage of being malleable both under normal use and within the context of vampire defense. It can be mashed, chopped, and combined with other elements to expand its deterrent properties to devastating effect. There are some recommended principles governing the use of garlic in order to maximize its effectiveness in vampire combat.

Use Fresh Cloves—Given their portability, convenience, and availability, you may be tempted to use dried powder or flakes in place of the raw product.

Do not succumb to this temptation. Dried garlic produces only a mildly irritating effect on your undead opponent compared to the fresh plant, and most dried products were produced in a factory setting some time ago; with each passing day, this dehydrated version loses its already compromised potency. If anything, use of garlic in dessicated form against your adversary will serve no purpose other than to enrage it, making it a more threatening opponent.

Separate and Peel—Although a whole head of garlic can serve to dissuade your vampiric attacker, a much more effective use is to separate the head into its individual cloves. When exposed to the air, peeled garlic cloves have a much stronger effect than those still encased in the layers of its parchment-like skin. Once split and peeled, garlic cloves have much more flexibility in their use, one of which is stringing them together to create a garland.

The Garland

Using a strong, synthetic material such as fishing line or thin-gauge wire, string a quantity of raw cloves end to end along the line, much in the same way you would thread a line of beads. The completed garland can then be tied around the neck or limbs to create an irritating and unappealing target for the vampire's attack. The type of material used to thread the cloves is important, as it will prevent the attacker from easily breaking the apparatus to separate it from your body.

Mince, Mash, Crush—Just as peeling a head of garlic into its separate cloves enhances its deterrent capabilities, crushing those cloves augments these properties even further. As garlic is crushed, the natural organosulfur compounds contained within the cloves are released; it is surmised that these compounds are the ones that cause the adverse reaction from your opponent. Fresh, minced garlic can also be combined with other elements to create a dispersal agent containing these vampire-caustic compounds. An example of a formula for creating a garlic-laced repellent follows.

GARLIC MACE-DISPERSAL AGENT

Ingredients

- 100 garlic cloves (raw)
- 4 quarts cooking oil
- 4 mason jars (quart size)

Directions

1. Peel and chop the raw garlic cloves until finely minced with a paste-like consistency.
2. Divide the minced garlic equally among the mason jars.
3. Fill each jar with cooking oil (use the least expensive oil you can find, as taste and smoke point do not matter).
4. Cap each jar and let steep at room temperature for at least sixty days.
5. Fill an empty spray bottle with garlic-infused oil mixture.

Once complete, the dispersal agent can be used during a vampire engagement as a deterrent to cause pain and distraction to your opponent. Although still not as potent as the single, raw garlic cloves, the steeping process allows a significant amount of the plant's compounds to infuse the liquid. The longer you allow the mixture to steep, the more potent it will become. Be careful not to substitute cooked or powdered garlic for the raw ingredient, and do not use water in place of oil; not only does the grease act as a catalyst for the garlic compounds, but its consistency enables the mixture to adhere well to any surface once sprayed.

IV. WEAPONS

Silver

Similar to garlic, silver causes an extreme reaction when used against the undead. The damage inflicted by this metallic element is similar to a chemical burn, and any vampire flesh that comes in direct contact with this metal will temporarily corrode and cauterize, causing a searing degree of pain to your opponent. In addition, silver seems to have the effect of dampening the enhanced healing abilities of the vampire, causing wounds that normally would close nearly instantaneously to remain open and painful.

When speaking of silver in terms of vampire combat, we must distinguish between the two readily available forms of this element:

Fine Silver—99.9 percent pure silver metal, this level of purity causes the most devastating reactions to the vampire's flesh, and is also a very soft and flexible element.

Sterling Silver—An alloy comprised of 92.5 percent fine silver and 7.5 percent other metal elements, most typically copper. While sterling silver does cause a reaction in the undead, it is nowhere near as extreme as when using the purity of fine silver.

As a weapon against the undead, silver does have its limitations. While many films have depicted undead hunters armed with lethal weapons crafted from this element, the reality is that silver is rather soft and pliable. The metal itself also cannot neutralize a vampire even if driven directly into the creature's heart, hence its categorization as a secondary weapon. The most significant disadvantage of using silver for your vampire arsenal is its price. While not as valuable as gold, silver is still considered a precious metal and has applications in decorative, commercial, and personal use. At the time of this writing, silver is priced at more than thirty U.S. dollars per ounce. Its value has also increased tenfold over the last twenty years, much more rapidly percentage-wise than the value of gold. Some have intimated that this dramatic increase in price is due in part to concerted efforts of the vampire species to drive up its value to minimize its availability to the public.

Due to its high price and malleable state, it is improbable for most citizens to forge vampire-neutralizing tools completely from pure silver. The best use of the metal in relation to vampire combat is to incorporate it as an enhancement to your existing arsenal, making each item that much more lethal to your opponent. This process of incorporating the metal into existing tools is known as "silver lacing."

Silver Lacing

Silver lacing can be accomplished in one of two ways. The metal itself can be smelted down, shaped appropriately, and incorporated directly onto the armament. The second and more practical method is to use the metal in its existing form as a necklace, charm, or bracelet and incorporate it into your arsenal by wrapping, interlacing, or stamping it into the implement or within any parts likely to come into contact with your opponent's flesh. A creative combatant can think of a variety of ways items can be laced with silver to make them exponentially more powerful in vampire combat. Some items in your vampire arsenal that do not normally contain silver and can be laced include:

IV. WEAPONS

Edged Weapons—Although knives, swords, and machetes are crafted from a combination of metal alloys, none contain significant quantities of silver to make them effective against the undead. Remedy this by applying silver to some portion of the blade that will make contact with your opponent's flesh. While it is possible to forge silver into an edged weapon, it is a complex and technical process. Only the most skilled bladesmiths should attempt to do so.

Stakes—While the wooden stake is the only weapon that can neutralize an attacking vampire with a blow to the heart, any other wound caused by this weapon to the vampire's torso will be minor at best and heal quickly. By lacing your stake with silver, you can boost the amount of damage caused by your weapon, in addition to preventing the vampire's wounds from healing rapidly. The open wounds can also serve as markers to allow you to adjust your subsequent strikes appropriately. Lacing a stake with silver can help provide some heft, weight, and reinforcement to a light and fragile weapon, enabling you to strike with additional force and momentum.

Restraints—As we will explore in the next section, there are a number of restraining devices that can be used in vampire combat should you need to contain or pin down a violent, writhing ghoul. Although hardy restraining devices can constrict your undead attacker's movements temporarily, lacing them with silver would boost their retention capabilities, and provide some reassurance to the captors that the attacker will be kept at bay for a greater length of time to allow for finishing the task at hand.

RESTRAINING EQUIPMENT

In most instances of vampire combat, your ultimate goal is to survive the encounter with your life unharmed and blood supply untainted. However, there may be instances where the need to control a member of the undead species becomes a necessity. This is particularly true if you are operating within a team to root out a suspected vampire nest in order to prevent further bloodshed and loss of life. While instances like this should be infrequent, educating yourself about which items are useful in containing a thrashing attacker is still valuable.

Paracord—Parachute cord, otherwise known by its abbreviated name, is a braided nylon rope that was used to suspend the chutes of skydiving paratroopers during World War II. Its synthetic construction makes it much more durable than ropes made from natural fibers, which are susceptible to rot. Outside of its original use, paracord is now commonly found in both military and civilian applications where a high tensile strength cord is necessary to ensure the safety of the user, such as in rock climbing, mountaineering, and rescue operations. In relation to vampire combat, paracord can be effectively used to create a restraining loop that can hold a vampire at bay. As with all devices used against this particular creature, care must be taken to account for the superior physical attributes of the species. Different grades of paracord have varying levels of breaking strength. For vampire containment purposes, only type III or IV paracord should be used.

Flex-cuffs—Also known as disposal restraints or cable ties, flex-cuffs are restraining devices made from nylon that function in much the same way as handcuffs, except much

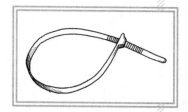

lighter, easier to use, and less expensive. Due to their low cost and high portability, flex-cuffs have become popular with military and law enforcement professionals, especially when the need to restrain groups of individuals arises. Flex-cuffs present several advantages over standard handcuffs in controlling a violent ghoul. Not only are they more cost effective, but they require less skill and time to deploy on a hostile assailant, a valuable asset when time is of the essence. When purchasing flex-cuffs for use in vampire combat, be sure to select the most appropriate type. Many different types exist to perform a variety of less strenuous tasks, such as securing wiring or binding nonthreatening items. When in doubt, purchase the same models used by law enforcement professionals, or choose the highest grade of cable tie available to you and use double the number when securing your undead attacker.

Ball Gag—A device often used for both restraint and entertainment, the ball gag can be equally effective against a resisting, aggressive vampire. Comprised of a synthetic ball attached to a leather buckle, ball gags are used to prevent an individual from speaking or, in an undead scenario, from attacking with bared fangs. Using a dedicated device for gagging purposes is much more effective than using a length of cloth or rope, from which the vampire may be able to extricate itself. Time is required to master use of this device in order to deploy it effectively against an attacking ghoul. Once it is tightly secured around the skull, however, there is little chance that your opponent will be able to continue its feeding assault.

Snaring Devices—Often used by animal control professionals, a snaring device can be as simple as a length of wire fastened to a metal rod. Snaring tools are commonly used to secure loose wild animals by looping the securing wire around the neck of the target and pulling it taut, minimizing the creature's mobility. This same concept can be directly applied to restraining a bloodthirsty vampire. Although simply designed, this tool can prove useful for several different applications in vampire combat. Not only can snaring devices be used to forcibly remove an attacking vampire from atop its human victim, the tool can also serve to pin a struggling ghoul to the ground and restrain its flailing limbs before delivering a neutralizing blow. Using a snaring device during an undead engagement does require a degree of expertise, and should be done only by individuals practiced in its use.

COMBAT REPORT: HECTOR SANTIAGO

Chef
New York, New York

I stand by the back entrance of Trattoria Del Sole, an Italian eatery in New York's Hell's Kitchen, where Hector Santiago, chef de partie, takes his smoke break. Dinner service is drawing to a close, which provides Santiago a brief respite from the chaos of a professional Manhattan kitchen to speak to me. Like many workers in the restaurant industry, Santiago is an undocumented immigrant.

He stands in the rear entranceway to the kitchen, keeping the door propped open with his foot as he blows smoke into the night

IV. WEAPONS

air. In one hand, he holds his cigarette; in the other, he wields his chef's knife, which looks to be of a custom design. Santiago was referred to me by Mama Cherie, his past employer and the New Orleans restaurateur I previously interviewed. He speaks fondly of her before we begin, although it is clear that their opinions differ greatly regarding the subject matter at hand.

Hector Santiago: Cherie's a wonderful person; a fair boss and a caring woman. A bit misguided, but very caring.

Vampire Combat Manual: She seemed to be a very compassionate person.
HS: History is littered with the bodies of those who felt compassion for their enemies.

I pause for a moment from my notes, taken slightly off guard by the poetic expressiveness of Santiago's words. He notices my hesitation and smiles.

HS: I received my master's in history from Universidad de Sonora in Mexico. I taught high school for several years before crossing over with my family. It is one of the myths that Americans have of Mexicans who come into this country— we are all uneducated illiterates capable only of making a living by lifting heavy things. Like most immigrants, we were looking for something very simple: a better life for our family. After 9/11, it was nearly impossible to do so legally, which is why we turned to our only alternative. Thankfully, many people in the restaurant business understand the situation.

VCM: It seems you had a falling-out with your former employer?
HS: Let's call it a difference of opinion. We do not share similar experiences with your subject matter, which is why I felt compelled to leave her employment. Let me tell you a story.

Six months after moving my family to New York from Louisiana, it was flu season, and the prep cook and a station chef called in sick, so I had to work a double that day. I spent the whole afternoon cutting and chopping vegetables and the rest of the night working two stations for dinner service without a single break. By the end of the night, I could barely stand. I didn't even bother to wash up, and just headed home to pass out.

I was walking toward the subway entrance when I felt the small hairs on the back of my neck stand up, the same way I imagine an animal feels when it senses its life being threatened. I looked around and saw nothing but fleeting shadows. I tried to shake the feeling, believing it to be simple exhaustion, but it would not subside. Suddenly, every fiber in my body told me to run. And run I did. I sprinted for three blocks, why and from what I did not know. I felt completely ridiculous, chastising myself even as I ran, but still, I could not deny my instincts. Finally, I stopped, completely winded and gasping for breath. I put my hands on my knees and tried to regain my composure, laughing quietly to myself. That's when it attacked.

Something grabbed me by the neck from behind and took my legs out from under me. I was being pulled into an alleyway, kind of like the one we're standing in now. I felt like a child. As much as I struggled, there was nothing I could do to fend it off. My body went limp, as if all the strength and will had left it. The pulling stopped, and the creature lifted me to my feet. Its face looked ordinarily human, not monstrous in the least. But there was something in its eyes that was terrifying; a combination of hunger, pain, and desperation. Its mouth opened and it leaned in toward my throat. I closed my eyes. That's when the image of my children flashed in my mind, and I knew I had to try to fight.

I pushed its face away with both hands as hard as I could. It let out a horrible screech and stumbled back. The flesh that came in contact with my hands looked blistered, as if badly scalded. I put my hands up again and the creature pushed past me out of the alleyway, disappearing into the night. I stared at my hands in amazement, and brought them close to my face. That's when I realized what made it retreat.

Santiago ducks back into the restaurant briefly, and comes back with something in his hand, which he tosses in my direction. It is a whole bulb of fresh garlic.

HS: During the day's prep work, I chopped an enormous amount of vegetables. Lots of *mirepoix* - carrots, celery, and onions. And garlic, bulbs and bulbs of raw garlic. In an Italian restaurant, it's common to use hundreds of cloves in one night. At the end of the evening, your hands stink of it. It is a smell that lingers; even after washing, your hands still feel tacky from the cloves. I used to find it unappealing, so much so that I considered changing cuisines. Now it's a scent that I look forward to every night.

Santiago finishes his cigarette, blowing the smoke upward toward the bright light of the full moon. He stares briefly at the night sky.

HS: I love this country. It has been very good to my family. If I could have come here through the proper way, I would have. When you face a choice of providing for your family or losing them to the *Narcotraficantes*, you don't have a choice. People do not realize the risks people endure to make it into this country. And I'm not just talking about the border patrols or the desert sun.

I read an INS statistic that said five thousand illegal immigrants cross over the border from Mexico into the U.S. every year. When I read that, I laughed. Multiply that number by a hundred and you're getting closer to the right number.

Why do you think our government would so greatly under-estimate such a number?

Santiago pulls closer to my face, as if revealing something he does not want others to hear.

HS: When you try to cross the borders, you must do it near sundown to avoid the heat and the risk of being discovered. The vampires know this. To those who are crossing, the crea-tures are known as *los demonios del desierto,* the "demons of the desert." When people disappear during their crossing, it's not the police that take them. And thousands are taken, often whole families. When the bodies are found, it's usually blamed on dehydration or wild animals, but we all know better. This says as much about the state of our country as it does the *de-monios* themselves—if so many are willing to still risk this fate, imagine how bad it is back home? We were very lucky, all of the group I traveled with made it alive. But as we walked, we heard many terrible sounds; sounds that I will take to my grave.

This is the United States, the most powerful country in the world. If the government really wanted to stop people from crossing their borders, do you not think they could do it? But if they stop the crossings, they stop the hunting. And if the hunters don't have the migrants, who do you think will replace them?

They say in America, the immigrant does the work that no one else wants. This is true. But we provide much more than the sweat off our backs to help this country. The truth is, by the sacrifice of our own blood, we keep Americans alive.

Santiago looks toward the kitchen as he hears his name being called by the head chef. He turns to me one last time.

HS: Write your paper. Spread your knowledge. But be careful, *hermano.* They are watching.

Using my body to shield his hand from view, he points in the direction of the darkened rooftops behind me. I slowly turn to look, but see nothing. When I turn back to address Hector, he is gone.

V.

COMBAT STRATEGIES AND TECHNIQUES

There is no hunting like the hunting of man, and those who have hunted armed men long enough and liked it, never care for anything else thereafter.

— ERNEST HEMINGWAY

aving detailed the physiological structure of your adversary and the selection of armaments that are effective against it, you may feel a sense of pessimism at your chances of surviving a vampire attack. This feeling is understandable—the physical superiority of your opponent is significant, and the weapons options are slim. However, the outcome of your combat engagement is far from a foregone conclusion. How is it possible that an individual can emerge victorious against an opponent that is superior in nearly every physical attribute? By employing the correct strategies to negate these advantages. Throughout history, from the legendary conflict between David and Goliath to Lawrence of Arabia's defeat of the Turks to the U.S. Special Forces and Northern Alliance's routing of the Taliban in Afghanistan, examples abound of lesser opponents defeating larger, stronger, better-armed enemies in battle by utilizing superior strategic tactics and techniques. This employment of strategy is no different when confronting the undead. In order to survive a vampire's lethal onslaught, you must apply your most effective weapon—your mind—and formulate a battle plan that shuts down your attacker's every advantage.

PRINCIPLES OF UNDEAD COMBAT

A critical aspect of defeating a vampiric opponent—more important than your choice of weapon or your method of attack—is the understanding of the fundamental principles of successful undead combat. Weapons can be lost, techniques can be forgotten, but if you have a deep grasp of the following basic principles, you can adapt your methods and strategies for any situation, as well as be able to improvise should things not work according to plan. While individual techniques are necessary to your success in vampire combat, their efficacy is augmented tenfold when coupled with the following principles:

LEVERAGE When confronting stronger and more powerful opponents, there is only one way you will be able to manipulate their body against their will: by employing the principle of leverage. Simply explained, leverage is the use of force  coupled with proper positioning against the weakest extremities of your opponent. Regardless of how much strength your attacker possesses, these extremities can only sustain so much weight. By effectively utilizing leverage, you can move your undead opponent in directions and force it into positions that are optimal for executing a neutralizing strike, despite its superior level of strength.

TIMING Like many things in life, in vampire combat, timing is everything. The best combat techniques in the world are worthless if they are employed at the wrong moment. It is necessary to train not only *how* to execute the proper strikes, but *when* to deliver them. Throughout a  vampire engagement, windows of opportunity will emerge to employ a technique that can end the confrontation. These moments are often sparse and fleeting. A strategic combatant not only takes advantage of these moments when they emerge, but learns how to make them appear.

POSITION Attaining the proper positioning can be a difficult principle to grasp, but key to your success or failure in vampire combat. Position can be described as the "invisible third

man" in any combat engagement. If used well, it can be a powerful force against your undead opponent; if used poorly, position can work in your adversary's favor. What makes this strategic aspect so difficult to master is the fact that the proper positioning is subtle in detail—placement of a hand slightly to the left or right of your target can make all the difference. It is also a trait that is not easily learned; you must develop what is known as a "feel" for your opponent, which often can only be acquired through hours of training and repetition.

STRATEGY Entering an undead engagement without a battle plan will leave you at the mercy of your attacker's own strategy. Unlike other types of undead opponents, the vampire is no fool. Not only is it effective at hunting, it knows itself and its prey very well; it is fully sentient regarding its own weaknesses, and will vigorously defend them from being exploited. We also know, however, that this creature can be reckless in its attack and arrogant regarding its perceived superiority over the human race. It is up to you to exploit these shortcomings. In vampire combat, employing an effective attack strategy is often seeing which opponent makes the first mistake. Ensure that it is not you.

SITUATIONAL AWARENESS

Before delving into specific tactics to address a vampire assault, we should first consider the environments where a potential undead attack could take place. In any type of hostile engagement, the setting of the encounter can be as noteworthy as the combatants themselves. This is particularly true when you are engaged with an adversary with attributes that surpass your own. Since you will enter the engagement from a physiological disadvantage, it is critical that you adjust your tactics to account for the external environment. In combat parlance, this insight is known as "situational awareness," and can be a crucial factor in surviving an undead attack.

Being attentive to your surroundings not only provides you with opportunities to survive the engagement; it may offer you an advantage you can utilize in eliminating your opponent. Although there is an endless number of specific external scenarios that can be analyzed, we will limit our discussion to those situations most commonly encountered by the everyday citizen.

Urban Environments

Of all the possible scenarios in which you may cross paths with a ghoul on the hunt, an urban environment is a common setting in our modern age. Metropolitan locations, with their high concentration of inhabitants in a densely populated area, are irresistible to most vampires. In addition to providing a rich feeding resource, urban environments are attractive undead habitation zones due to the network of subterranean passageways, drainage systems, and viaducts that make underground travel during daylight hours possible for the creatures, should the need arise.

Preparing for combat with a vampire in an urban setting is no easy feat. The increased presence of law enforcement in metropolitan areas can be an asset, but also it may be difficult to remain armed and ready in the event of an attack. Depending on the city, regulations on personal protective armaments may be so stringent that a weapon intended for vampire defense can be construed as menacing not only to the undead, but to innocent humans as well. It is advised that you consult local regulations on personal protection to ensure that you are in compliance with the laws governing your region. Thankfully, most municipalities do not have specific limitations regarding typical vampire combat implements—stakes, silver, and garlic.

One additional point must be made about the behavior of citizens in urban surroundings. Should you find yourself engaged in combat with a member of the undead in a densely populated metropolis, do not assume that any calls for assistance will be met with immediate attention by neighboring bystanders. Longtime residents of an urban environment are often wary of involving themselves in unknown and threatening situations, lest they risk putting themselves in harm's way. This phenomenon is prevalent enough that it has been analyzed by social psychologists, terming it the "bystander effect" or Genovese syndrome, named for the renowned criminal case exhibiting this condition, the murder of Kitty Genovese.

In the winter of 1964, Catherine "Kitty" Genovese was returning to her home in Queens, New York, when she was attacked by an assailant, who stabbed her twice in the back. Despite her cries for help, no one came to her aid. The shouts of a concerned bystander eventually drove away the attacker, only to have him return a short while later to finish his assault, stabbing Genovese several more times, raping, and killing her. While there is some claim that the original lack of response from her neighbors was exaggerated, the Genovese murder to this day is still cited as a warning to victims that your cries for help may go unheeded. It is for this reason that many recommend avoiding calling, "Help!" and instead screaming, "Fire!" as the latter may bring a more curious and responsive crowd.

Rural Environments

Facing a vampire in a rural environment presents an entirely different set of challenges than confronting one in an urban setting. While you will not have to contend with the possibility that your armaments may be confiscated by law enforcement, you will also not have the luxury of being in a densely populated area where others may come to your aid.

One of the greatest risks of being attacked by a blood-sucking ghoul in natural surroundings, such as the country-side, farmlands, or a vast empty field, is the fact that you will be not only isolated from other people, but also far removed from any type of safe haven or retreat. It is imperative that you try to minimize your travels after sunset should you find yourself in an unfamiliar rural setting. Should evening travel be unavoidable, here are some recommended tactics to avoid being targeted for consumption by a ravenous vampire:

- **Stand Ready**—Since you are in an environment not be frequented by law enforcement, you can prepare in advance by having your armaments in hand as you set off on your travels. It is advised that you keep both hands filled with some type of weapon, be it a stake or a bladed weapon. Keeping vulnerable regions on the body covered by some type of defensive barrier, such as heavy clothing or more formal protection, is also advised.

- **Travel Quickly**—The longer you remain exposed in a rural environment, the more likely it is that you will be attacked by a stalking creature of the night. It is suggested that you travel using some form of mechanized or animal transport, such as an automobile or motorcycle or on horseback. Should none of these options be available to you and you must travel on foot, travel as fast as possible to your destination, maintaining a pace that you are able to sustain for the entire duration of your trip. This is another situation in which your cardiovascular fitness level can affect your ability to survive. Your goal is not to outrun your undead attacker, but to minimize your exposure time in a high-risk environment.

- **Keep Moving**—There are essentially two methods of attack that a vampire can initiate in a rural environment: a blitz or an ambush. Both of these types of attack require the victim to be exposed in the open for a significant duration. Regardless of your level of fatigue, hunger, or exhaustion, do not pause for any length of time during your travels. Even the briefest of respites opens the door for your attacker to assess your vulnerability and set the stage for its assault. It should go without saying that, if at all possible, do not travel alone. Speak to no one you encounter during your evening travels. Should you be traveling on foot, do not accept any transportation assistance offered by strangers; while arriving at your destination faster due to the offer of a good Samaritan seems like a safe strategy, there's no telling if the individual is in fact a vampire or one of its accomplices—until it is too late. Should you absolutely need to rest during your journey, do so under the shelter of a confined space, such as a house, barn, or stable. While not completely secure, the enclosed space minimizes your exposure to both nature's elements and the undead.

- **Stick to the Road**—While you may experience a feeling of extreme vulnerability while traveling alone on a desolate path, it is imperative that you maintain travel on designated roads. In an open environment such as a road or highway, your field of vision is extremely high, allowing you to monitor any unusual movements in the distance and limiting an attacker's ability to initiate a stealthy assault. In areas crowded with brush, tall grass, or foliage, it is much more difficult to assess a threatening situation, and much easier to fall into an ambush. Rest assured, a vampire will leverage any and all natural conditions to improve its chances of a successful hunt.

SEASONAL CONSIDERATIONS

The season during which the engagement occurs can be equally as significant as the environment. The variations in seasons throughout the year are created as a result of the axial tilt of the earth and the hemisphere that faces the sun at a particular point in time, with the hemisphere pointed at the sun experiencing more daylight.

The effect of seasonality in a vampire combat scenario is twofold: the external temperature at which the engagement occurs, and the hours of daylight during the normal day. Depending on the time of year, your strategies and tactics for vampire combat can change dramatically. Although there are four distinct seasons, the seasonal differences can be divided into two distinct groups relative to an undead engagement.

Autumn/Winter—As the temperature drops, the greatest concern you must address in undead combat strategy is the waning hours of available daylight. During the winter months, you may experience several hours less of daylight than during the peak summer months, culminating in the winter solstice, the longest night of the year. The most significant threat of the early-setting sun is that it often occurs before the close of the workday, resulting in many more people traveling in darkness as they make their way home for the night. It has been rumored that within certain vampire communities, the hours between five P.M. and seven P.M. during the winter months are known as "the butchering hours."

Thankfully, all is not in your adversary's favor during these harsh cold months. The lower temperatures require individuals to dress in several layers and warm, heavy outerwear, keeping the most at-risk areas of the human body under wraps. The need to wear heavier clothing also affords you the ability to conceal armaments, such as a hardwood stake or silver-laced blade, more easily on multiple areas of the body.

Spring/Summer—With the shifting of the seasons to the warmer, temperate months comes a new set of issues related to vampire combat. As the first bulbs begin to flower, signifying the onset of spring, be aware that you must adjust your undead strategies appropriately. The daylight hours will gradually grow longer, a tremendous benefit in minimizing your risk of being attacked. No longer will you need to anxiously watch the sun setting in the horizon hours before your actual workday ends. As daylight stretches longer into the evening hours, you can be secure in the fact that you can safely make it home long before the undead emerge for their nocturnal pursuits.

When it comes to the warmer seasons, however, not everything works to your benefit. Although the longer days mean more outdoors time available, the favorable weather increases the temptation to remain outside long into the night. While it is not recommended that you live a hermetic, antisocial existence, be cognizant of the fact that while you relish the comfortable summer moments, there are those who also benefit from the warm night air for more insidious reasons.

Another issue to be mindful of during these months is the sparse amount of clothing you will wear. Whereas in the colder months, you bundle yourself under several warm layers, you will probably find yourself slipping on nothing more than a T-shirt and short pants for much of the summer. While comfortable and necessary in the oppressive seasonal heat, this level of attire makes concealing a vampire weapon on your body all but impossible.

V. COMBAT STRATEGIES AND TECHNIQUES

Additionally, the lack of clothing leaves all of your primary target areas exposed and ripe for a vampire's assault. For those of you residing in areas where a temperate climate is the norm, this must be a year-round consideration. Although you could don protective gear to guard these target areas during the warm seasons, the attention drawn by the combination of summer attire and defensive shielding would probably be too conspicuous to bear. As you find yourself outdoors past sundown during temperate seasons, make sure you adhere to the precautions listed previously, and keep fully aware of strangers in your surroundings.

Daylight Saving Time

An additional seasonal element that must be considered is the time-setting practice known as daylight saving time (DST). Followed throughout the world, although in increasingly smaller numbers, DST is the practice of moving the time forward one hour during the spring and backward one hour during the fall. The history of modern daylight saving time has been commonly explained as a method of energy conservation established during the early twentieth century. However, an alternative theory for the origin of this practice also exists.

It is publicly acknowledged that widespread adoption of DST occurred during the years of the First World War by both the Allies and the Central Powers. Germany and its allies first carried out the practice in 1914, with Britain and its European partners shortly following suit. By 1918, Russia and the United States had adopted the practice as well. The rationale provided to the general public for the adoption of

DST was as a means to conserve energy and reduce electricity use for the wartime effort by extending daylight into the evening hours. What is less known is that during this same time period, undead assaults throughout these same regions increased at an exponential and alarming rate, particularly in areas of the globe directly involved in the war effort. Research has shown that throughout history, vampires naturally gravitate toward regions in turmoil due to the convenient and accessible availability of prey, particularly those involved in hostile conflict. It has been hypothesized that while the public explanation provided for the switch to daylight saving time for a majority of the modern world was to benefit the war effort, the truth may be that it was developed as a solution to benefit neither the Allies nor the Central Powers only, but the entire human race against a more ominous, global threat.

While some may believe this vampire-based theory to be farfetched, it is also a fact that since its adoption in the early 1900s, forces have been at work to alter and repeal daylight saving time throughout the world. The practice has been adopted, repealed, and re-adopted throughout history. Currently, most of the world has either abolished or failed to implement the practice; North America and Europe are the only continents where it is nearly universally practiced. It is also important to note that within the Continental United States, Arizona is the only state that currently does not enforce DST; it also happens to be the state with one of the largest populations of illegal immigration in the U.S. While seemingly unrelated, there may be an underlying significance to this relationship *(see Combat Report: Hector Santiago)*.

Daylight Management

A primal strategy employed by animals in avoiding lethal predators is being aware of the times when their adversaries are on the hunt, and minimizing their exposure during these hours. In vampire combat, this translates to reducing your exposure in public after sunset. While it is often unavoidable to interact with the outside world once darkness falls, it is also important to maximize your productivity during daylight hours so as not to place yourself at undue risk. This can be done by rigorously managing your time from the moment the sun rises until it disappears into the horizon.

The best way to be certain of how many daylight hours you have at your daily disposal before your safety is jeopardized is to be precisely aware of each day's sunrise and sunset, down to the exact minute. Fortunately, there are many assets available that can make this tracking easy and stress-free.

Technology—There are a plethora of electronic tools, timepieces, and online resources that can provide accurate information on the precise time of each day's solar activity. For most individuals, this can be the primary method used to track the hours of light available in order to plan your day. However, caution should be taken on becoming over-reliant on such technology. While these tools will be effective a majority of the time, there is a likely chance that, at some point, technology will fail you. Electronic devices may malfunction, or you may find yourself in an area inaccessible to online resources. It is during these times that familiarity with alternative daylight assessment methods is a must. Just as a soldier is taught land navigation with a rudimentary map and compass even though sophisticated GPS devices are at his disposal, so too must you be able to manage your time in the daylight without depending solely upon technology.

Forecasts—In the same way we now rely on electronic devices to inform us of the weather at any present or future date, forecasters, astronomers, and farmers relied on a publication titled *The Old Farmer's Almanac* to do the same hundreds of years ago. First published in 1792, the *Almanac* relies on a secretive, proprietary methodology to accurately calculate a variety of weather forecasting data. An unsubstantiated rumor is that although its original intended use was to assist with farming activity, the *Almanac* was also used for the purposes of daylight management against the undead. While some elements of its predictability may be questioned, the publication's ability to provide accurate sunrise and sunset times still makes it a powerful, non-technological resource. At the very least, a printed resource such as the *Almanac* can act as a backup to any powered device you use to provide the same information.

Eyesight—Should neither of the resources above be available to you, do not despair. There is a method to calculate the number of hours remaining before the sun sets without the use of any external tools or devices. Although not the most accurate of methods, it can provide you with an estimate upon which you can assess your ability to find a safe haven while still in daylight. Looking into the sky toward the sun, place the fingers of either hand just below it, so that the top of your fingers just touches the bottom curve of the sun. Count the number of fingers between the bottom of the orb and the straight line of the horizon.

V. COMBAT STRATEGIES AND TECHNIQUES

Each finger represents approximately an hour's worth of daylight. Thus, if the sun is three fingers from the horizon, you have three hours in which to operate before the darkness arrives. Due to the inconsistency of this technique, you may want to overcompensate and estimate thirty minutes less than the time calculated using this methodology in order to ensure your own safety should your calculations be incorrect.

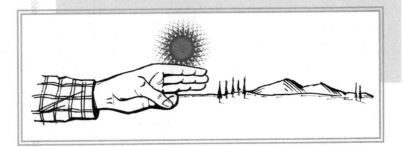

ASSESSING YOUR OPPONENT

Like many predators, a vampire will often initiate its attack with speed and without warning in order to minimize its energy expenditure and maximize its hunting success. Due to the swiftness of its attack, you may not have a moment to fully assess your adversary prior to its assault. Should you find yourself having the time to take stock of your opponent before battle, there are small visual cues to note that may aid you in determining the threat level and difficulty of the impending assault.

Pallor

A vampire's superior physical attributes are often dictated by the frequency of its feedings, or lack thereof. Your opponent will by default have a pale complexion, a side effect of the transformation process resulting from the creature's recurring need to replenish itself. However, the longer a vampire goes without feeding, the more pallid its outward appearance will become. The longer this period, the more strained and pale its appearance, a consequence of the blood being drawn from the extremities to sustain its internal systems. This is a significant observation. The degree of pallor can serve as an indication of the strength levels of your opponent and the length of time since its last feed.

Posture

Just as an assessment can be made of your opponent based on its complexion, so can it be done by observing its posture. While the digestive system of a vampire is extremely efficient, it is also notoriously cannibalistic. Should its feeding requirements not be met, a vampire will begin rapidly devouring itself, inciting the change in complexion just discussed as well as causing it to develop "postural kyphosis," or a hunched back. The longer the hunger goes unsated, the worse this symptom will appear. A vampire unable to feed will literally begin to fold in on itself until it becomes nothing more than a deformed ball of undead, thirsting flesh.

Stature

When entering any undead combat engagement, you should always assume that you have a strenuous and taxing encounter ahead of you. There are some details, however, that may help formulate a better strategy against your undead opponent depending on its size and girth.

Short Opponents—Vampires that are smaller in stature often use their lower center of gravity to their advantage, and attack the foundation of their victims by taking them off balance and forcing them to the ground before initiating their feeding attack. The best strategy against a shorter vampire attacker is to avoid being taken to the ground by your opponent. Make an effort to keep the engagement on the feet, where you may have a better ability to keep your attacker at bay with your reach advantage.

Tall Opponents—Vampires with superior height will utilize their reach to ensnare their victims with their long limbs, often wrapping their hands around their victims' throats and throttling them unconscious before they even have a opportunity to counterattack. While the effective strategy against smaller vampires is to keep the fight standing, against taller undead opponents, the best strategy is to try to bring the engagement to the ground, where much of their reach advantage can be neutralized.

Heavy Opponents—Much like a stout human opponent, a vampire with a greater amount of girth will use weight to its benefit. A larger vampire opponent will look to overwhelm you with its size, almost certainly by a smothering type of blitz attack. Although the creature is still faster than any human opponent of equivalent size, this mass will also affect the creature's speed and mobility. Much like a matador must contend with a charging bull, the best strategy against heavy vampires is to evade their rushing attack rather than meet their force head-on, and launch your own counteroffensive.

Thin Opponents—Already equipped with a superior level of speed, the slender vampire is that much faster than your average bloodsucker due to its lithe physique. Creatures with less physical mass are unlikely to resort to a blitzing attack; instead, the slim undead will look to use their quickness to confound their victim when they are ready to strike. The best strategy against a thin opponent is to eliminate the possible angles for their attack by aggressively pushing toward your opponent, or placing your back against an object or structure so that the creature has limited ability to flank or circle around you and surprise you from behind.

HUMAN VULNERABILITIES

In order to successfully defend your own body against assault, knowledge of your own anatomy is critical, as there are specific targets that have shown to be consistently favored by the undead during their hunting expeditions. These targets are directly related to the concentration of blood flow throughout the human circulatory system. Although a vampire can siphon blood from any laceration, it will look to target an area that enables it to draw the maximum quantity of blood in the minimum amount of time, which translates into targeting one of several major arteries in the human body.

Carotid Arteries—The target area most frequently associated with vampire attack, the carotid arteries

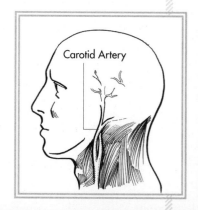

Carotid Artery

are located along both sides of the human neck, close to the surface of the skin. Popularly depicted as the sole target of a hungry vampire, there is good reason for these areas to be a preferred feeding site. Not only are the arteries easily accessible given their proximity to the surface of the epidermis, this region is also usually unobstructed by clothing, unlike other major arteries on the human body. It is for these reasons that this is a highly vulnerable area on the human body, one that can be quickly accessed via a single, accurate bite from a skilled succubus.

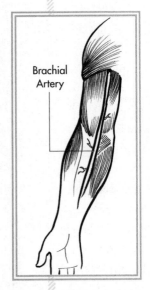

Brachial Artery

Brachial Arteries—An area commonly used by medical practices for test sampling and pressure gauging, the brachial arteries are also favored targets for a vampire's attack. Running the length of the upper arm, the prime location where a vampire looks to open blood flow is the area on the opposite side of the elbow, alongside the biceps tendon. Of all potential targets for an undead attack, this is the least popular due to the impediment of clothing covering the area as well as the ability of a human to effectively defend this region by pressing the forearm closed toward the biceps.

Femoral Arteries—The target area least suspected by victims during a vampire assault, the femoral artery is an ideal strike target due to the speed and quantity of blood flow. Located along the interior portion of both thighs, it is one of the largest arteries in a human being and supplies blood to the lower half of the body. Due to its location below the heart and its gravitational effect, it is the artery with the highest pressure of blood, and is often used to palpate an individual's pulse rate when the radial or brachial arteries cannot be located due to low blood pressure. Once ruptured, a bleeding femoral artery can cause an individual to lose consciousness in less than a minute, with death from blood loss following shortly. Despite it consistently being covered by clothing, it is still a susceptible target. A single swipe from the nails of an attacking vampire can open up this bloodline on an unprepared victim.

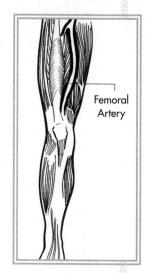

Femoral Artery

Latching

Once your undead opponent is able to locate and home in on one of these three primary targets, it will secure its mouth over the region, inflict a wound large enough to release the arterial blood pressure, and initiate the exsanguination process, draining the victim of his or her blood. This process of securing and opening the target wound is known as "latching."

It may seem like a hopeless situation once a vampire latches onto your body and commences the feeding process. While the circumstances are certainly dire, the engagement is far from over. Remember that a bite from a vampire is not a death sentence. Provided that you are able to unlatch your opponent from the wound and dress it in a timely fashion to staunch the blood flow, you can survive the engagement. The creature's ability to secure and latch a target also seems to come with experience—vampires with a lack of hunting expertise will take longer to latch effectively, providing you an opportunity to avoid the threat and launch a counterattack. The older and more experienced the vampire, the more effective its latching skill. Unfortunately, it is difficult to discern between novice and veteran vampires until you are already engaged in combat.

V. COMBAT STRATEGIES AND TECHNIQUES

ENEMY ASSAULT TACTICS

Just as there are diverse types of vampire classes, many variations in attack strategies are employed by these classes. Some of these variations are dependent upon the specific vampire class initiating the attack, but other external factors can also influence the assault methodology, including environment, terrain, and desperation of the vampire itself in its desire to feed. While subtle deviations also exist in the attack formations, vampire assault tactics generally can be broken down into the following categories.

The Blitz

Blitzing is the most common method of attack encountered by humans during a vampire assault. It is almost universally employed at some point by all vampires, and often comes with little to no warning, the goal being to shock the victim into immobilization and secure a latch before there is an opportunity to counter the attack.

While the direction of the attack can vary, there are four general types of blitz attacks you will most likely encounter.

FORWARD BLITZ The forward blitz occurs when your adversary confronts you head-on. While the vampire loses much of the surprise element in this attack, it can generate a significant amount of fear and anxiety in its victim when approaching directly from the front, freezing its victim in his tracks. Often a vampire will approach calmly as if just a normal passerby, then launch its attack at the last possible moment. It is for this reason that you should always be mindful of the neighboring population in your immediate vicinity once darkness falls.

Forward Blitz

FLANKING BLITZ The flanking blitz occurs when the vampire attacks from either the left or the right side of its victim. As the undead attacker is outside of the victim's primary sight line, there is an element of surprise generated by this attack. Mindful combatants who are peripherally alert and aware of their surroundings can prevent themselves from being caught off guard by a flanking blitz. Should you find yourself caught unaware by a blitz coming from this direction, make every attempt to turn into and face your opponent so that you can adequately defend the assault and prepare your own offensive.

Flanking Blitz

V. COMBAT STRATEGIES AND TECHNIQUES

AFT BLITZ Of all the blitzing maneuvers, the aft blitz is the most hazardous to the victim, due to the significant element of surprise generated by the vampire, the unanticipated nature of the attack, and the severe impact made by the creature on the startled victim's body. In this scenario, the creature is initiating its assault sequence from the rear, completely out of the target's line of sight. Once contact has been made, the vampire will look to retain the element of surprise by bringing its victim to the ground and securing a mounted position on the back, where it can proceed to attack any one of the major arteries.

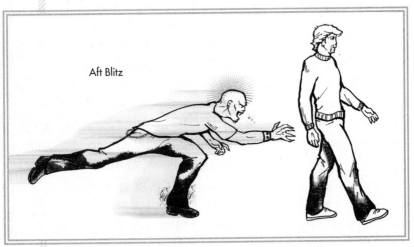

Aft Blitz

AERIAL BLITZ An unusual tactic not often utilized in densely populated areas, the aerial blitz is encountered in environments where large structures abound. In this blitzing attack, the vampire secures a high position from atop a mounted structure, such as tree branches in a wooded area, or fire escapes or building scaffolding in an urban location. It will then time its assault with the passing underneath of its unsuspecting victim. Given the way this attack method is executed, the aerial blitz may also have given rise to the mythology that

Aerial Blitz

vampires are capable of flight. This type of attack requires the greatest amount of skill on the vampire's part, as any mistimed attack will result in a victim fully aware that it is in jeopardy. If successful, this aerial maneuver is effective in generating a successful feed due to the shock and awe factor and the sheer impact of the creature's body onto the victim.

The Stalk

While the majority of vampires will attack their intended targets without warning or advance notice, there are some within the species that will hunt their victims by tracking them down in an extended pursuit, known as a stalk. While the vampire risks the loss of its target during a stalking

V. COMBAT STRATEGIES AND TECHNIQUES

pursuit, some creatures enjoy initiating this complicated game of cat and mouse.

The rationale for utilizing a stalking tactic in lieu of the much simpler blitz method is not completely clear. During a stalk, a vampire will initially make its presence known to its intended target, causing it to flee and commencing the pursuit. Due to the victim's awareness of being pursued by an unknown entity, the "fight or flight" response mechanism is triggered in the human body. This response causes a variety of chemicals to be released into the bloodstream, including adrenaline, noradrenaline, and cortisol. The body also will divert blood from the internal organs to the muscles in the limbs, in order to prepare the body for some type of physical response, be it fight or flight. It has been hypothesized that some vampires enjoy feeding on this elaborate mix of chemicals in the bloodstream, hence the riskier and more complex tactic of the stalk. The rapid increase in the victim's blood pressure and heart rate also facilitates a quicker feeding session once the vampire has secured its prey.

The Seduction

A tactic used almost exclusively by the Seducer vampire sect, seductions employ cunning, flattery, and manipulation rather than violence and physical force. As can be inferred from its moniker, vampires who employ this tactic will seduce their targets into becoming willing victims with little to no struggle, including welcoming the creature into their home, where all the household inhabitants are at risk. Creatures employing this strategy often do so in the guise of a human looking for companionship. Some vampires are skilled enough to target specific individuals, let their undead status be known, and convince the victim outright to become a feeding source. This type of seduction often comes with the promise of being turned into a member of their species. These promises often go unfulfilled. The most common locations for seductions to take place are social establishments such as restaurants, nightclubs, and taverns, but they may also take place at seemingly innocuous locations such as centers of worship, libraries, and university campuses.

The time required to fully complete a seduction varies depending on the creature and the gender of the intended target. Seductions involving female victims typically require twenty-four total hours to complete, often ending at the victim's residence. Those involving male victims are often completed within three hours, frequently culminating in a random location such as a vehicle, alleyway, or bathroom stall. This marked discrepancy of time and location speaks more to the dynamics of human relationships than to the seductive skill of the vampire itself. Due to the time required to complete a seduction, this method is often a secondary tactic used to supplement the more recurrent feeding requirements of a ravenous ghoul.

The Deception

In a strategy used with much greater frequency in decades past than in today's society, vampires have employed the use of deception similar to the way hunters do in order to ensnare prey. Historically, this tactic was utilized by vampires whose lair was located in a rural area, off the beaten path from human pedestrian traffic. There are two basic types of deceptions that are employed by the undead to entangle an unsuspecting victim.

- **Ambushes**—Deceptive traps based on some type of physical ensnaring mechanism, such as a deadfall or a trip wire, are known as ambushes. These traps require the target to trigger a component on the trapping mechanism, resulting in his ensnarement. Ambush devices used for hunting purposes by the modern-day vampire have become limited, but not forgotten. These trapping devices are now often utilized by the creature to protect the surroundings of its lair from would-be trespassers and vigilante "vampire hunters." Explanations of the most common types of ambush traps will be detailed in the section on team-based combat.

• **Hoaxes**—Deceptions that create a false scenario in order to lure an intended victim are known as hoaxes. These scenarios often involve another individual, either the vampire itself or a human accomplice. In a hoax scenario, the victim is made to believe that he is assisting the individual in some fashion (i.e. providing physical assistance, clarifying directions) when in reality, the stage is being set for the victim to become the evening's feast. Like ambushes, hoaxes are used most often in locations where human contact is sporadic. While most vampires will employ a much more direct, hostile approach in hunting their victims, some continue to employ a hoax strategy for their own personal amusement, as a diversion from their more forceful methods, or in order to avoid unnecessary physical risk while securing their prey.

COMBAT REPORT: KATE WOLCOTT

Vampire Hunter
Minneapolis, Minnesota

It's been thirteen months since I first interviewed the vampire once known as Christine Wolcott. It has taken me that long to track down the whereabouts of her sister, Kate. Shortly after Christine's disappearance, Kate became estranged from her family, and has also undergone a transformation of her own. From my network of sources, I have learned that Ms. Wolcott has joined the ranks of self-described "fang stalkers," those who intentionally target members of the undead species for termination. My interaction with her is the closest I was able to come to achieving my objective of locating members of the Blood Assassins.

Among vampire hunting teams, Ms. Wolcott is known as a baiter, or "lamb." Operating with a small tactical team, it is her responsibility to draw the target into an open, vulnerable position so that the other operators can execute a coordinated ambush. It is the most hazardous of roles among stalkers, as she must place herself in the most helpless of positions—prey for a thirsting vampire. Her early years as an athlete and martial artist have served her well, as her reputation among my sources as one of the best baiters in North America precedes her.

We sit atop a building across from where this evening's operation is to take place. Ms. Wolcott begrudgingly allows me to spend a few moments with her as the rest of her team moves into position. She is stunningly beautiful, and looks very similar to her image in her sister's photograph, with the exception of a dramatic streak of red dye running through her blond hair and a look of world-weariness in her eyes. She is dressed appropriately for her role tonight, in a formfitting black microdress and alluring heels, accentuating her athletic physique. Her demeanor plays in sharp contrast to her seductive appearance.

Vampire Combat Manual: I'm sorry about your sister.

Kate Wolcott: Christine was always sensitive, even as a baby. I used to tease her something terrible, as older siblings do. Rather than fighting back, she would always fall to pieces and go running off to Mom to be rescued. As we both grew older, I told her that she needed to toughen up, that Mom wouldn't always be there to help; otherwise people would just walk all over her. But she was just too thin-skinned, too trusting. Too naïve about how the world can really work.

As she got older, I knew Chris was having a tough time growing up in our home. It's not easy when you have an older sister in general, but she had it rougher, thanks to our mother. Mom always wanted her to follow in my footsteps—honor roll, track and field, martial arts—but she just never realized that even though we were less than three years apart, Chris was a very different person. When she began running with that alternative crowd, it really threw Mom for a loop. We were your normal boring suburban family: soccer games, meat loaf night, reality television. The friends that Chris brought around not only didn't fit that mold, they pissed all over it, and our folks just couldn't handle it. The more our mother tried to pull her in my direction, the more Chris pushed toward her own path.

VCM: What did you think of that path?

KW: I had no problem with Chris's friends or that particular scene. Everybody needs to find a place in this world, and if she found it in that group, it was fine by me. I met many of her friends, and when you take off the makeup and change out of the clothes, they're no different from anyone else. My mom couldn't accept that fact, though, and asked me to keep an eye out for her, especially when she was on her own. I looked deeper into the clubs Chris and her friends visited. That's when I discovered something much more threatening.

In the past few decades, the gothic scene has skyrocketed in popularity. What was once a niche explored by a few has now become part of mainstream culture. In nearly every city and every town in America, you'll find a club that hosts some night that caters to this crowd, and for good reason. It may sound completely ludicrous and conspiratorial, but the darker truth is that although this rise in popularity was meant to look organic and natural, it has, in reality, been completely manipulated by those who have the most to gain: the ones who feed on us. This scene attracts some of the most sensitive and vulnerable youth, exactly the type of victim they desire. Why hunt down your prey when you can have them willingly open themselves up for you? I knew they were responsible for what happened to Chris. They're like a virus, a plague; if you don't stop it early enough, you may not be able to contain it. And it's only getting worse. They must be stopped; otherwise it won't just be people like Chris who are the victims.

VCM: How did you become a baiter?

KW: The more I learned about how they hunt, the more I realized that they are no better than us. Stronger and faster maybe, but no better. People have just been brainwashed by this bullshit mystique surrounding them. The reality is they are just as gullible as any creature blinded by desire—desire for power, for sex, for money, and, in their case, the desire for blood. One of the reasons I've been successful is because I haven't allowed their sham of a reputation to affect my psyche. That's what they count on, you know. PsyOps is the technical term—the psychological element of combat. Take that away, and you've stripped away at least half their power, and then it's just a matter of being a smarter fighter.

One of the keys I've discovered, what's made me so good at what I do, is understanding that as a baiter, it's all in the timing. There's a brief moment, just before they are about to feed, when the creatures lose virtually all control of themselves. I refer to it as the "golden moment." The anticipation of the blood is too great, dampening most of their senses. That's the time to strike. It lasts for only a few critical seconds, but if you pay close enough attention and get the timing down, a few seconds are all you'll need. I was hoping that this insight would bring me to the attention of a certain group of like-minded individuals, but unfortunately I've had no luck yet.

Wolcott is clearly referring to the Blood Assassins. It was my hope that she would be my gateway into the organization, so I try to hide my disappointment. I decide to refrain from telling her the specifics of my meeting with her sister, and instead remove the framed photograph and letter from my satchel.

VCM: I believe she wanted you to have this.

Wolcott takes the frame from my hand. Her eyes crease upon seeing the photo. She slowly tugs the envelope free from the back of the frame, and removes the letter contained within. She reads quietly to herself. A smile crosses her face as she flows through the page. Her eyes begin to well up, and she swallows hard. Suddenly, her sadness seems to harden, and she stares intensely at what her sister has written. She folds the letter neatly and puts it into her gear bag.

A quiet crackle comes over her transceiver; her teammates letting her know they are in position. Wolcott depresses the receiver twice, confirming that she's ready to move in. She hands me a pair of high-powered binoculars, points toward an open alleyway across the street, and departs. Twenty minutes pass. Finally, Wolcott comes into view with her target in tow. She runs her hand through her hair alluringly, the streak of red clearly visible through the optics. I watch as she seductively pulls the creature into the alleyway. She plays her role impeccably, as her target looks completely oblivious to its own vulnerability. She allows it to pull the back of her hair and turn her neck to the side. I watch closely as the vampire rears up and opens its mouth.

Just as the creature is about to bear down into her flesh, I notice a moment when its eyes roll back into its head, revealing just the whites. The golden moment. At this precise instant, Wolcott reaches into her small clasp bag and pushes a large silver globe into the creature's mouth. She clips two heavy leather straps studded in silver and connected to the sphere around the creature's head, securing the device into its mouth. At the same moment, her teammates appear, two enormous men. They loop an animal snare around the creature's shoulders and pin it to the ground.

Wolcott stands over the vampire. A teammate tosses her a machete and, without a word to the creature, Wolcott severs both its arms at the elbows. Her teammates pull the limbs aside. She begins to speak, and although I am unable to hear her exact words, it is clear Wolcott is interrogating her attacker. The creature shakes its head back and forth, having difficulty communicating with the restraint in its mouth. Wisps of smoke float above the creature's mouth and nostrils, a result of the silverized globe in contact with vampire flesh. Wolcott takes a small dagger from her teammate and begins to make small incisions in the creature's torso. Before the wounds can close up, she plunges whole cloves of garlic into the cuts underneath its skin. The creature's screams continue to be muffled by the gag. I adjust the focus on the binoculars to zoom in on Wolcott's mouth as she continues her interrogation, and I am able to read a single word from her lips: "Gregor." The creature continues to shake its head.

Wolcott retrieves a stake from her operations bag. As she stares directly into the vampire's eyes, she sinks the weapon into the creature's heart. Her actions look slow and purposeful, as if *she is intentionally prolonging the moment. The vampire's eyes widen and the stake pushes deeper into its body. Suddenly, the creature releases a choking yelp and begins to spontaneously combust. The team watches as the body disintegrates into a pile of ash and gelatinous liquid. Wolcott stands, looks up toward my position for a brief moment, and then departs the scene with her team. I never speak to her again.*

DEFENSIVE TACTICS

Having reviewed the various ways your opponent may initiate its attack, we can now focus on the proper countermeasures should you find yourself in a compromising situation against a bloodthirsty ghoul. Given your physical disadvantage, it is ill advised that you try to match your opponent's strength with your own. Rather, the key to mounting an effective defense against an undead opponent is to utilize techniques that do not require immense power to execute successfully.

Keep in mind that the objective in any vampire encounter is not to "win," but to survive. Your opponent is not looking for money, jewelry, or material possessions. It looks to accomplish a single objective: to feed. The following techniques can enable you to prevent that from occurring, and ideally provide you enough time to mount your own counteroffensive.

THE CROSSGUARD Recall that one of three primary regions a vampire will target is the neck area, looking to open one of your carotid arteries. By utilizing a blocking maneuver known as the Crossguard, you can shield this region from your opponent's snapping fangs. Raise your arms toward your chest and cross your wrists at your throat. Place the backs of your hands directly against the sides of your neck, with your palms open and facing outward. Keep your elbows and forearms tight against your chest as you guard your open neck with both hands. The reason for crossing your arms and guarding your neck with the opposite hands rather than simply cupping your hands over your own neck is so that you can fend off any oncoming attacks by pushing away with your palms. Cupping your own neck with your hands also leaves you open to a vampire covering your hands with its claws and strangling you with your own fingers.

THE L-FRAME The goal in vampire defense is to take advantage of your body's natural attributes to counteract your opponent's assault. One of the ways to accomplish this is to ensure that your attacker does not have the opportunity to close the gap between its fangs and your bloodlines. The most successful methods utilize your skeletal structure as a rigid obstruction against the

vampire's oncoming force. One such method is known as the L-frame. Should you find yourself face-to-face with a hungry adversary looking to pull you into its jaws, lift your elbows and place them squarely on your opponent's chest. Your forearms should be bent ninety degrees with your hands against the vampire's neck, forming the shape of an *L* and controlling the direction of its mouth. This technique enables you to create adequate space between yourself and your attacker by utilizing the strong humerus bones in your upper arms to "frame" against your opponent. Despite the forceful pressure of your attacker into your body, your arms and elbows can provide the critical barrier necessary to prevent the vampire from closing the distance to complete its attack.

THE SPRAWL An indispensable technique learned in amateur wrestling, becoming proficient in the sprawl is essential to preventing an attacking ghoul from dragging you to the ground. In vampire combat, the sprawl not only serves as a maneuver to counter a takedown attack, it also provides a level of protection to the femoral arteries in the legs by moving them out of harm's way. This technique is most effective against a frontal blitz attack, but can also be effective in countering blitz assaults from the right or left flank. As your opponent rams into you with the intention of pulling you to the ground, drive your legs backward and force your hips down toward the ground. By keeping the base of your legs wide and your center of gravity low while leaning the weight of your body onto your opponent, you can avoid being put in a compromising position. When done correctly, a sprawl can enable you to be on top of your opponent even if driven to the ground, where you can mount a quick counterassault.

THE VISE Also commonly known as the "closed guard," this technique is a key ground-fighting position in Brazilian jiu-jitsu that enables you to use your weight and leverage to your advantage, even when you are in the adverse position of being underneath your attacker. Should a vampire be able to pull you to the ground during a combat engagement, wrap your legs around the waist of your undead opponent and clamp your legs around its back, hooking them together at the ankles. There are a plethora of techniques and maneuvers that can be executed from this position, but at the very least, the vise enables you to use the strength of the most powerful muscles in your body—your quadriceps, hamstrings, and gluteus maximus muscles—to control your attacker and keep it from closing in on your target regions.

Those of you with ground fighting or BJJ experience may wonder, why the need to rename this technique when it is already universally known as the "closed guard"? The renaming of this technique is a conscious and intentional decision. Changing the naming convention reminds those experienced practitioners that you cannot simply transfer existing human combat techniques into undead combat without accounting for the unique characteristics of your opponent, and that doing so may cost you your life. Remember that despite the

humanoid appearance of the creature you are engaging, very few of its traits remain human when it comes to combat.

THE BULL GRIP A unique hold developed exclusively for vampire engagements, this technique serves several purposes. Like the L-frame technique, the Bull Grip prevents your attacker from closing the distance. It also enables you to control and mitigate the use of your opponent's primary weapon, its fangs. As the vampire closes in for an attack, brace your arm against its throat, forcing the ulna bone in your forearm upward and underneath its chin. With your free hand, grasp the back of your opponent's neck region. You can also grab a handful of your attacker's hair should it be within reach. Using the hand of the arm underneath the chin, grab your own forearm to secure the position. By using the powerful leverage and framing created by both arms as well as securing the attacking weapon, you can prevent any further damage from your opponent's snapping fangs. This technique works best when you are assisted by another combatant, who can deliver a neutralizing blow while you maintain control of your attacker.

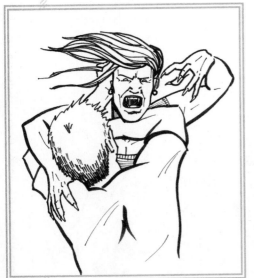

OFFENSIVE TACTICS

An intelligent warrior once said, "The best defense is a good offense." In vampire combat, it is critical that you take these words to heart, as you will need to have an effective attack strategy to end an undead engagement. It is a sad fact that the longer you remain engaged with a vampire in hand-to-hand combat, the less likely it is you will survive. Once engaged, your goal should always be to end the battle as soon as possible before you expend all of your energy, because there is no question that you will tire before your opponent.

One of the most challenging aspects of vampire combat is that it often is a contradiction of intentions—you must keep certain defensive areas away from your opponent, but also draw close enough to attack its vulnerabilities; you must protect yourself against the vampire's bite, but you must also pull it into you so that you can launch a counterattack of your own. It is due to these contradictions that strategy, tactics, and proper technique are so essential to emerging successful and alive from a vampire engagement.

Ineffective Tactics

Before we explore the methods you can use to neutralize your undead attacker, it is valuable to cover the techniques that are wholly *ineffective* in a vampire engagement. It is critical that you internalize the difference. During the heat of battle, you may instinctively revert to one of these tactics by force of habit, expecting to cause an incapacitating reaction in your opponent. Should you make this error, the only body withering after such an attack will probably be your own.

- **Strikes**—All forms of direct strikes whether from the fists, feet, elbows, or knees, are largely disregarded by an attacking vampire. Striking blows are effective against human beings due to their ability to cause several reactions: a shock to the nervous system, concussive force to the brain, or damage to the internal organs. In the vampire species, none of these reactions has any dramatic effect. The only purpose a strike could possibly serve against a bloodsucking opponent is to put a slight amount of distance between two combatants.

- **Chokes**—Any technique that employs a form of choking, whether it is an oxygen-depriving throttle or a blood-blocking strangulation, is useless against a member of the undead. These methods will not work for the simple fact that your adversary depends on neither oxygen nor blood flow to the brain for survival. Any choking technique employed on your opponent will fail, leaving you depleted and vulnerable.

- **Pressure Point/Nerve Strikes**—Questionable in application even against a human opponent, targeting pressure points on a vampire's torso is not advised. Beyond the fact that being able to apply such strikes requires a level of skill and experience available only to a known handful in the entire world, nerve clusters on a vampire do not operate the same way as they do on an unconverted human. Even simple blows to common nerve centers, such as those used in boxing strikes that render a human unconscious, are ineffective against an attacking ghoul.

- **Ocular Attacks**—While it may seem like a good idea to target the visual organs of your undead combatant, it is not a recommended tactic. Not only is it difficult to deliver a strike that could incapacitate your attacker even for a moment, but the vampire's natural healing ability makes it so that even significant injury to the various components of the eyes, such as the corneas or lenses, is repaired shortly after the damage has been done.

- **Joint Locks**—Although it is possible to break the bones of an attacking vampire, the pain threshold exhibited by the species is much higher than any human being's. In addition, the superior healing factor of your attacker makes it able to withstand most joint-breaking attacks, the bones healing themselves in short order. This being the case, techniques such as arm bars, knee bars, and wrist locks are not recommended.

- **Groin Strikes**—Severely incapacitating to a human attacker, blows to the groin go unnoticed by your undead opponent. While not yet scientifically confirmed, it seems that the sexual organs of a vampire lose not only their intended function, but their sensitivity as well post-conversion.

Targeting the Heart

As depicted in film and television, it would appear to be an easy proposition to drive a sharpened piece of lumber through the chest of a vampire. Combat reality, however, is much different from fiction. Before we begin to explain techniques that you can perform in order to effectively strike this critical organ, it is imperative that you first become completely familiar with physical details surrounding this target area. Luckily, the location, position, and the skeletal structure surrounding the vampire heart remain unaltered during the transformation process. We need only examine the human anatomy to obtain the information necessary to target this vulnerability in undead combat.

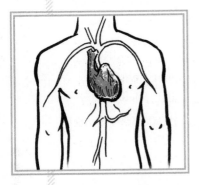

Location—A common misconception is that the heart lies farther toward the left side of the torso, under the pectoral muscle. The primary reason for this misconception is the placement of our hand over the area we believe to be the heart during formal rituals and ceremonies. In actuality, the heart is closer to the center of the upper chest, just slightly left of the spinal column. Study the corresponding illustrations carefully and strive to develop a sense of the organ's location on opponents of various sizes, heights, and girths. With practice, you will be able to pinpoint this attack location from just a quick glance at your adversary's torso.

Size and Position—It is essential to become familiar with estimating the position of the heart on a vampire torso from a variety of directions. In combat, you will need to make quick yet accurate judgments of the positioning based on the height and width of your attacker in order to determine the optimal way to strike the target. On an average vampire, the center of the heart is positioned approximately six inches from the base of the throat and ten inches from the left side of the torso. The heart itself is approximately the size of a fist, roughly five inches in width and ten inches in circumference.

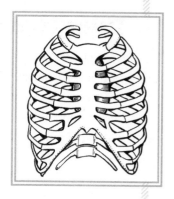

Protective Anatomy—Ideally, this target would lie just under the surface of the epidermal layer, easily penetrated by a slight jab of your weapon. If only it were so easy. Given the magnitude of importance to both human and vampiric bodies, the heart is heavily guarded from external damage. The organ is encased within the anatomical structure known as the thoracic cage, commonly referred to as the rib cage. This bony structure is what makes striking the heart directly so difficult. The front of the rib cage, called the sternum, obstructs direct access to the heart almost entirely. The upper seven ribs are connected to the sternum via costal cartilage. The spaces between the ribs, known as the intercostal spaces, also contain the intercostal muscles and nerves. Given this anatomical barrier, your strike must be either powerful enough to cause the surrounding defensive structure to collapse or precise enough that your weapon slips between the skeletal obstructions. The level of muscularity or girth of your opponent may also interfere with your ability to strike deep enough into the chest cavity.

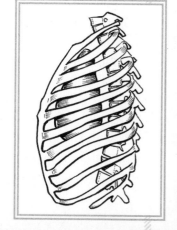

V. COMBAT STRATEGIES AND TECHNIQUES

Staking Tactics

Untrained individuals copying what they've seen in the media as their sole source of information may believe there is only one way to drive a stake into a vampire's heart during an undead combat engagement. In fact, there are several different methods by which you can strike this vulnerable mark. How you decide which tactic to use will depend on several factors; distance, body position, weapon placement, and combatant strength are all variables that come into play when determining the ideal staking tactic. When you commence your training, be sure to practice all of the various maneuvers below. As you grow in proficiency with these techniques, you will begin to instinctually recognize which method is suitable to use against your undead adversary in a given situation.

CROWNING STAKE The most well-known method of staking attack, the crowning stake is executed by holding the weapon in the ice-pick or reinforced ice-pick grip and driving it forcefully through the chest into the target. In order to execute this technique successfully, you must either shatter the sternum with your weapon or slide between the intercostal spaces of the third through sixth ribs close to the center of the chest.

Tactical Details: While the crowning stake is the most popular of all the staking techniques, it also can be one of the more difficult to execute. This maneuver requires a significant amount of power to execute successfully. The key to ensuring that you deliver a powerful enough strike is to visualize striking far deeper into your opponent than necessary. Your intention should be not just to tap the heart, but power through it. It is also not uncommon for your strike to be diverted from its path by a skeletal obstruction, missing the target entirely, and

Crowning Stake

there is the remote chance that your weapon will snap before reaching its target. Ensure that your stake is sharpened, hardened, and made from the proper raw material to avoid combat failure. Employing the crowning stake also places you in the risky position of being directly in front of your opponent, leaving yourself open to attack; be certain to make your first strike count.

RISING STAKE An effective attack that requires much less power than the previous technique, the rising stake avoids the bony structures of the sternum and rib cage entirely by traveling beneath these skeletal structures to attack the target organ. Grasping the weapon in the hammer grip, place the tip of the weapon pointing upward toward the lower portion of the rib

V. COMBAT STRATEGIES AND TECHNIQUES

Rising Stake

cage, close to the solar plexus. Force the weapon straight upward and underneath the rib cage. Using this technique, you avoid the power necessary to break through the skeletal structure, requiring less energy in your attack.

Tactical Details: When employing the rising stake, be alert to the fact that the distance the stake must travel to tap into the heart is greater than when using a direct crowning stake attack. This greater distance must be compensated for by employing a longer weapon. In order to facilitate an accurate strike, keep your wrist straight and point the tip of the stake up during the thrusting motion as you penetrate the vampire's flesh, driving upward with the intention of reaching all the way to the base of the throat. This technique also requires you to drive the weapon through the powerful core muscles in the abdominal region, which may necessitate the use of some force.

Should your hand turn during the attack, there is a strong likelihood that your strike will miss the organ. Never assume that simply because you have driven your weapon to the hilt into your attacker, you have struck your intended target.

FLANKING STAKE This staking tactic is especially effective in situations where your undead opponent's arms are raised, exposing target regions under the armpits. The flanking stake is also one of the few techniques where both the ice-pick and hammer grips can be utilized with equal efficacy. Rather than attacking your target straight through the chest and having to crash through the thoracic cage, this method approaches the target from the side of the body, sliding the weapon between the ribs. Once either side of your opponent's flank is exposed, drive your weapon into its torso. The stake will enter the chest cavity, pass through the lung, and penetrate the heart.

Flanking Stake

Tactical Details: While the flanking stake requires less strength than the other two methods described earlier, it does call for a greater level of precision. For this technique to be effective, the stake must slide between the ribs in order to reach its target. The ideal entry point for your weapon is between the fourth and fifth rib, approximately one inch below the armpit to the immediate side of either pectoral muscle. As you approach the target, ensure that your weapon is level and parallel to the ground when you strike; a blow that is angled improperly upward or downward is likely to career off one of the ribs that protects the heart. Given the direction of your attack, make certain that your weapon is adequate in length to travel the distance from the side of the body deep into the torso.

ASSASSIN STAKE The most secure method of neutralizing a vampire given the direction of the attack, the assassin stake, as its name implies, approaches the target from the least noticeable direction, directly behind your opponent. This technique not only circumvents the need to penetrate the front of the chest cavity, but it also reduces exposure to your opponent's primary weapons—its fangs and claws— and limits the potential for a counterattack. Visualizing the location and size of the heart on your opponent, drive your weapon deep into its back. An ideal blow will slide between the intercostal space of the fourth, fifth, or six ribs, penetrating the heart from the rear.

Tactical Details: Like the other attack methods, there are details worth noting in assassin stake that can affect the successful execution of this technique. Because your visual cues will be different when confronting an opponent from the rear, accurately pinpointing the heart from behind may be more difficult. Facing the back of your opponent, your attack region will be the upper left quadrant of the torso, approximately six inches from the base of the neck just to the left of the spine. The other obstacle faced during a rear assault is the surrounding anatomy; while you no longer need to worry about penetrating the sternum, you still must ensure that your weapon avoids the surrounding skeletal structure. An imprecise blow may also strike the wide, triangular bone known as the scapula, or the shoulder blade. Depending on your adversary's physique, the back can also be a heavily muscled area, requiring you to strike with a higher degree of force in order to penetrate the trapezius muscles covering the target area. Nonetheless, this rear approach can be as effective as a crowning attack from the front of your attacker while being far safer for the human combatant.

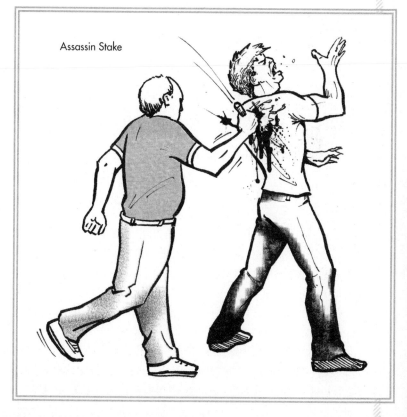

Assassin Stake

Decapitation Tactics

Another offensive tactic available when confronting a member of the undead is the separation of its head from the rest of its body via a decapitating strike. Once separated from its torso, the vampire head ceases to be an active threat, and should be destroyed immediately. Should you want to avoid a close quarters confrontation with a member of the undead, decapitation can be a viable alternative, provided you are trained in this technique.

While it is our intention to remain objective with respect to the various undead combat tactics, we will point out that given the choice, most combatants should utilize a staking tactic over decapitation. The rationale for this is twofold. First, a decapitation strike requires the use of an appropriate weapon, which is often unavailable to the combatant if the attack comes unexpectedly; not many civilians are able to carry a large-bladed implement on their person throughout the typical day. Stakes, on the other hand, can be concealed on the body with relative ease. Second, and more important, the ability to deliver a decapitating strike to an agile, moving target is much more difficult than normally thought. Even the most skilled swordsman would find it a challenge to deliver such a blow, never mind a poorly trained civilian. Although a lengthy explanation of specific decapitating techniques is beyond the scope of our discussion, there are some general guidelines you can follow should you be interested in utilizing this method.

- **Slice and Dice**—Rather than chopping at your attacker's neck as if you were attempting to fell a tree, imagine slicing through it as if it were a large tomato. By pulling the blade through the target with controlled force rather than awkwardly hacking at it, you are more likely to slice deeper into the vampire's neck, with the purpose of severing the head in a single blow. Be sure to follow through completely on your swing, much like you would when swinging a baseball bat or tennis racket, using a smooth, powerful stroke.

- **Don't Get Fancy**—A mistake frequently made by untrained civilians wielding a bladed implement is imitating techniques seen on film or television. With no formalized training, individuals often resort to copying what they see on the big screen. Do not make the same error; to do so only reveals your lack of expertise. Twirling, whirling, and spinning your blade like a baton-wielding drum major serves no purpose other than to expend needless energy and risk the loss of your weapon. Such maneuvers do nothing to intimidate your opponent; if anything, it generates the opposite reaction. Experienced swordsmen display an economy of motion, moving when necessary and attacking only when the time is right.

- **Train with Masters**—Should you truly be interested in focusing on decapitation as an offensive tactic, it behooves you to seek out formal instruction in blade-based combat. Kenjutsu, Silat, and European swordsmanship are examples of arts that emphasize the use of the blade in combat, and they can educate you in the proper form and technique with such weapons. Without such formal training, it is unlikely that you will survive many encounters against rampaging ghouls using a decapitation strategy alone.

It is not our intention to dissuade you from employing any particular technique against your opponent, especially if you find yourself skilled in such a method. However, if you at all question your ability to perform such a challenging maneuver on a mobile vampire, it is perhaps best to reserve this technique for situations where your opponent is secured, immobilized, or in a deep slumber from the previous night's blood feast.

COMBAT STRATEGIES

Beyond the detailed knowledge of your opponent's anatomical vulnerabilities and the techniques used to exploit them, there are additional combat strategies you can employ to enhance your lethality and expose your opponent's weaknesses during any vampire engagement. On the surface, these strategies may seem excessive or unnecessarily violent. Keep in mind that in undead combat, you are always the underdog. Any tactic that provides even a slight edge can help balance those odds, and hopefully tilt them in your favor. Once you have mastered the basic staking techniques, study the following strategies to deepen your vampire combat skill set.

The Snakebite

As we have described previously, there are several critical elements of a successful staking attack: analyzing your opponent's anatomy, pinpointing the heart, and driving your weapon into the organ. Should you successfully complete all of these components, the engagement is over. However, a stake that misses its target leaves you in a position susceptible to your opponent's counterstrike. Improve the odds of neutralization by employing a strategy called "the snakebite," otherwise known as "triple tapping."

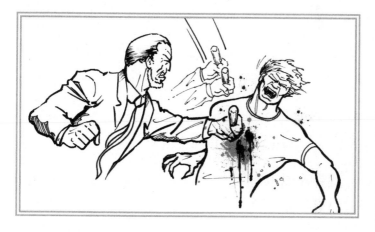

Watch a venomous serpent launch an attack and you'll note that it often strikes not once, but several times, inflicting damage with each bite. The concept is similar in the snakebite. The purpose of this technique is to ensure that your blow has struck its intended target, the vampire heart, and to not relent until you know for certain. Rather than rely on a single thrust of your weapon, strike your target several times in rapid succession. Although you can strike as many times as you feel necessary, three is the average number of hits typically executed within a realistic time frame against an undead opponent. This technique is a variation of a firearm strategy known as the Mozambique Drill, where three shots are fired to ensure attacker neutralization: two shots in the torso and one shot to the head. In this instance, your weapon will be your staking armament, and all three blows will be directed to a single target.

Given the number of times you must strike your opponent, speed is of the essence in the snakebite. Do not pause between strikes to assess whether you have struck your target; simply continue until the three blows are complete. A question that is commonly asked regarding this strategy is: "How will I know if I have struck the target?" You will know it when you see it. The chain reaction caused by a neutralizing blow to the vampire heart is immediate and unmistakable; once struck, your opponent becomes instantly immobilized as a chemical reaction is triggered from interaction with elements present in the wood and the cellular structure of the vampire heart, ultimately resulting in a near-spontaneous combustion of your attacker.

Blood Baiting

A hungry vampire is a dangerous vampire, but also a reckless one. Should the creature's feeding cycle be interrupted, it becomes increasingly violent in its quest for sustenance. It also, however, will react with increased carelessness, especially when it senses that a source of food is near. Use this erratic behavior to your advantage by baiting your opponent into putting itself into a compromising position, allowing you to end the confrontation. One baiting technique used to great success by experienced vampire combatants is the matador.

The Matador

1. Before squaring off against your attacker, create a small incision on the palm of your hand. The exposure of your blood to the open air in the vicinity of a thirsting vampire should create an immediate reaction. Allow the blood to pool in your palm as you confront your opponent.

2. As your attacker draws near, extend your palm outward and away from your body. You will note that your opponent is uncontrollably drawn to the wound. While your opponent's attention is focused on your exposed cut, ready your weapon in the opposite hand. Prepare for the vampire's imminent attack.

3. Your attacker will launch itself at your exposed hand. Pull your wounded hand back and away, and pivot around your opponent as it strikes, continuing to keep your palm extended from your body.

4. Strike the attacker's heart, either using the flanking or assassin staking technique. Repeat as necessary.

Dismemberment

While not a finishing technique per se, dismembering your attacker can be a very effective deterrent strategy. Striking such a blow may cause the creature to abandon the engagement altogether. Severing limbs from your opponent's torso, however, is often much easier said than done.

Recall that your opponent has a superior advantage when it comes to its curative abilities. Any strike with a bladed weapon that does not completely sever its target, but instead causes a cut or lacerating wound, will heal quickly. Even deep gouges in the creature's flesh will repair itself within minutes. A vampire, however, does not have the ability to regenerate a limb once it has been severed. Thus, the most effective type of strike with a bladed armament is one that slices through its target, separating the appendage. While strikes of this nature will rely on a sharp blade and an aggressive attack, there are strategies you can employ to make a dismembering strike more successful.

I. **Attack the Appendages**—Whenever there is talk of dismemberment, the first target of choice inevitably is the head. While it is true that separating the vampire head from its torso will neutralize the threat, it is also one of the most difficult maneuvers to perform. A much better strategy is to target the smaller appendages on the body such as the forearms, wrists, and lower legs. While a vampire without a hand can still effectively attack, it will probably abandon the struggle, realizing it is contending with a trained, fearsome combatant.

2. Split the Joints—Even with a razor-sharp weapon, slicing through human bone can be difficult to do in combat, particularly if you are untrained in such a specialized skill. Given that your attack must be accomplished quickly, pinpoint areas on the body where the bones meet at a synovial joint: elbows, wrists, knees, and ankles. Given our skeletal structures, it is much easier to slice through these targets than it is to cut through solid areas of bone such as the femur, tibia, fibula, radius, and ulna bones. Much like a butcher breaks down an animal at the flexible joints, so too should you take advantage of this element of human anatomy.

3. Don't Stop Slicing—Another novice mistake when it comes to executing a dismembering attack is pausing to determine whether your strike was successful. In the time it takes to admire your handiwork, not only may the wound repair itself, but your opponent is likely to launch a counterattack of its own. Thus, you must strike accurately and repeatedly at your target in order to successfully slice through its limb before it can attack. There is absolutely no reason to pause after striking; it will be abundantly clear whether your strike was successful or not by the appendage lying on the ground.

De-latching

You may encounter an instance during a vampire engagement when your attacker is successful in securing a latch on to your body. While this puts you in an extremely precarious position, do not panic. Recall that a bite from a vampire is not a death, or undeath, sentence. You can survive, provided you act quickly and purposefully. The longer you remain latched, the greater the risk of unconsciousness due to blood loss. The advantage you have is the fact that once latched, a vampire's focus will be on drawing sustenance from the wound, with little regard for anything else. Using the proper technique, you can break free of your attacker's jaws by using the following de-latching method.

The Prybar

1. Secure a close-combat weapon (i.e. knife/stake) in one of your hands and plunge the weapon into the cheek of your attacker.

2. Rotate your weapon backward and forward in a circular motion, cutting as you move. Drive the implement deep between your opponent's jaws.

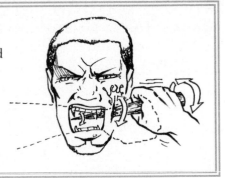

3. Using the weapon's leverage against the jawbone of your attacker, wrench open its jaws just wide enough to separate its mouth from your body, just as you would open a clamped object.

As distasteful and brutish as this technique may seem, you must strike forcefully, particularly during your attempt to pry open your opponent's mouth. The clamping strength of a vampire's jaws is superior to that of a normal human. Only an equally aggressive counterattack will enable you to free yourself from an aggressively feeding vampire.

ADVANCED COMBAT TACTICS

Once the fundamental staking techniques have been mastered and combat strategies studied, you can begin to merge them with more complex combat maneuvers. As you advance in your training, you will begin to grasp how particular techniques work better in certain situations and against specific types of assault. The ultimate goal of any combatant is to be able to recognize and apply the appropriate counterattack relative to your adversary's movements. In time, your skills will become intuitive and dictated by your undead opponent's assault pattern. While attacks can vary wildly, the following are some effective counters to the most common types of undead engagements.

The Stakewrap

An excellent counter to a forward blitz attack, the stakewrap enables you to control your opponent, even if for a brief moment, allowing you to fixate on your target and launch a counterattack.

1. As your opponent drives into you, wrap your non-staking arm around your opponent's neck, securing the head in a fixed position. Grab hold of your own clothing to secure your grip around its neck.

2. Drop onto your back and wrap your legs around your opponent in the vise grip.

3. With your opponent temporarily immobilized, raise your weapon, pinpoint your target's heart, and drive the stake deeply into its back.

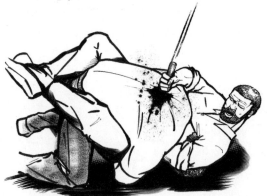

The Impaler

The impaler is particularly useful in instances when your opponent is holding its torso close to your own, making it difficult to generate sufficient force for a staking attack from the front.

1. As your opponent secures itself to your torso, prevent a latch and create space between you and your opponent by framing your arm against its neck.

2. Secure the stake in your hand, and place the tip in the approximate location of the heart directly on the back.

V. COMBAT STRATEGIES AND TECHNIQUES

3. Drop forward and slam your opponent's back to the ground, driving the stake into the heart from behind. If your blow is accurate, you will immediately feel your opponent release its grip. Be sure to brace yourself for impact to ensure you do not fall onto the point of the protruding weapon.

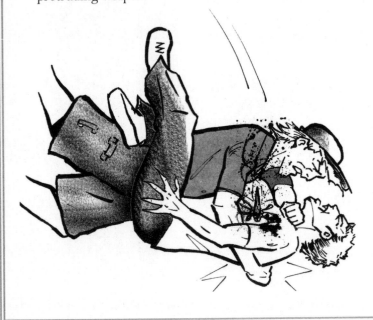

The Sprawl and Stake (SAS)

A technique that is well suited to those with strong takedown defense, the SAS not only keeps you from being dragged to the ground by your opponent but also takes advantage of the creature's exposed target area during its assault.

1. As your attacker drives into you during its initial attack, spread your lower body backward in a sprawling maneuver.

2. Drop your hips to the ground, forcing the weight of your upper body onto your opponent, preventing it from grabbing hold and lifting your body in the air.

3. Raise your weapon and drive it into the heart target area on your opponent's back. Repeat as necessary.

UNARMED COMBAT

There is no question that the most dangerous type of vampire combat is facing off with your opponent completely empty-handed. Unluckily, it is also a common occurrence for many unprepared victims. The vampire is an intelligent hunter and will always look to attack its prey at their most defenseless. The time may come when you find yourself facing a bloodthirsty ghoul without a defensive implement at the ready. This leads to one of the most difficult of vampire encounters: unarmed combat.

We will not mince words regarding this type of undead encounter: In unarmed vampire combat, it is unlikely you will survive. Your opponent is simply much more physically dominant, and will likely overpower you should you not have the means to end the engagement. As we've noted previously, there are very specific methods by which you can neutralize an attacking vampire, all of them requiring some type of armament, be it a stake for a blow to the heart, a bladed weapon for a decapitation or dismemberment attack, or the lethal rays of the sun. Without any of these at your disposal, your goal in an unarmed encounter is not to neutralize your attacker, but simply to survive its onslaught.

In armed combat, many of the techniques detailed previously (the L-frame, the vise, the bull grip) are utilized to set the stage for a neutralizing blow. While their use in unarmed combat can effectively prevent a vampire from latching on to your bloodlines, it may only be a matter of time until your strength gives out. Thus, it is more important to focus on broader concepts to help you avoid and survive this most perilous of vampire encounters.

Always Be Armed—While it may be stating the obvious, the fact is that the best way to avoid confronting a vampire without a defensive implement is to always have one prepared. The most common argument against such advice is the notion that carrying around a wooden stake on a daily basis is not only impractical, but borders on paranoia. What is ignored by this argument is that a long, sharpened stick is not the only weapon you can prepare in case of vampire attack. A necklace or charm of pure silver or a handful of garlic cloves in your pocket provides some level of defense against a ghoul with minimal personal inconvenience. While you may not be able to neutralize your foe with such deterrents, you may at least make your attacker think twice before proceed with the assault.

Do Not Run—Should an encounter with a vampire be imminent and you find yourself without a weapon, a pointless course of action would be to run from your assailant. By now you realize that a vampire has all the physical abilities to give chase and overcome your pace. Unless you are moments from your residence, where a vampire is unable to continue pursuit, a much better strategy than running is to conserve your energy and position yourself optimally for the attack—with your back facing a wall to avoid a blindsided assault—and scan the area for items that could be used as an improvised weapon.

Look for Weapons—As stated in the previous point, the best use of the moments before engaging with your undead opponent is to search for some type of implement to assist you in your unarmed encounter. Depending on the environment, you may be able to find or design an improvised weapon. Tree branches, table and chair legs, or slats from a wooden crate can all function as a de facto vampire stake should a proper tool be unavailable. The key to creating a makeshift weapon from found items is to try make it such that one end looks imposing enough to penetrate your attacker's heart. Often merely wielding such an implement will make your attacker realize that you are an educated opponent, and pause to consider its choice of target.

Remember to Breathe—Here is another seemingly obvious point, but it absolutely bears noting for the majority of individuals who have never experienced close combat, vampire or otherwise. Once engaged in battle, several bodily functions will occur: Your heart rate and blood pressure will elevate, your breathing will become hurried, and your senses will adjust so that the body's primary focus is survival. What often occurs in untrained individuals is that they are so focused on engaging with their opponent that they unconsciously hold their breath; this behavior will have serious deleterious effects on your ability to defend yourself. Hold your breath long enough while engaged with a vampire, and your opponent will not have to worry about subduing you; you will have done it to yourself. The best way to breathe while in the midst of combat is to take in air slowly for a count of three through the nose and exhale it just as slowly through the mouth. Not only will this help to calm your elevated heart rate; it can also prevent hyperventilation. Fending off a bloodsucking ghoul is challenging enough; do not make it that much easier for your attacker.

Get Some Attention—There is only so long that you can engage unarmed with a succubus before your strength level drains to the point that the creature is able to overpower you. Thus, it is in your best interest to try to end the encounter as soon as possible, the ideal way being to draw the attention of others to your predicament. As noted earlier in our discussion on Situational Awareness, an effective way to draw the public's attention is to scream, "Fire," rather than, "Help." Another important point to make is to not let ego impede your ability to look for assistance. Screaming as loud as possible is not weak or cowardly; it is intelligent and strategic, given the nature of your opponent and the threat it poses to your life.

V. COMBAT STRATEGIES AND TECHNIQUES

DISABLED COMBATANT TACTICS

As difficult as a vampire combat engagement can be for a healthy individual, it can be that much more challenging for someone with a physical disability. Ordinary citizens already begin a vampire engagement at a physical disadvantage compared to our undead adversaries; any additional vulnerability can make an individual that much more susceptible to a vampire's attack. The undead often perceive a disabled person as an easy feeding session, one that is unlikely to cause difficulty or execute a counterattack.

Disabled combatants, however, should not be disheartened at the prospect of engaging a vampire in battle. A well-trained combatant who acknowledges and compensates for his disability is better prepared to effectively handle the situation than an able-bodied individual with no training. The key to success for disabled combatants is to examine how their disability may affect their combat performance, and to adjust their methods accordingly. The following are general observations for those with common disabilities when confronting a bloodsucking attacker, and some recommendations to compensate for those disabilities.

Blind Combatants—As an individual who must operate without sight, a blind combatant is already acutely sensitive to his surroundings in order to manage normal day-to-day activity. This instinctive sensitivity is even more critical when it comes to vampire combat. Your undead opponent will use your lack of sight as an opportunity to launch an attack when you least expect it via a blitz-type assault.

Blind combatants, however, also have several traits that may prove useful against a bloodsucking ghoul. First, you may have the advantage of being readily armed before an attack commences; a wooden walking cane used for guidance can prove to be an effective improvised stake when the need arises. Second, as with many disabled individuals, the deprivation of one particular sense may enhance the ability to focus on the remaining active senses. Although you may not see your attacker coming, you may be able to hear its rapidly approaching footfalls. You may also be cognizant of odors that other humans would overlook, a useful trait should your undead attacker be downwind of you. Third, you are already accustomed to operating in darkness, which is likely where a vampire attack will occur.

As a non-seeing individual who must neutralize a hostile ghoul, the most important combat traits to develop are your anatomical awareness skills and sensitivity. Without visual cues to pinpoint the staking target location, you must do so using the sensitivity of your hands and other non-visual cues when engaged with your attacker (i.e. location of the mouth relative to the undead heart). Thus, it is critical to train with a variety of partners in order to be able to feel your way to your attacker's heart to strike a neutralizing blow.

Deaf Combatants—Deaf combatants have a particularly difficult situation in a vampire engagement. Not only will you lack the ability to hear your attacker approaching; you may also, depending on the extent of your disability, not be able to cry out, limiting your ability to call for assistance. However, your lack of hearing is probably the least impactful of all disabilities when it comes to undead combat. You are still able to pinpoint attack targets, watch for hazardous situations, and be mindful of your vulnerability as you watch the sun set into the horizon.

Much like individuals without sight, deaf combatants can develop acuity in other senses in order to compensate for the disability's affect in combat. As you will not hear your attacker approaching, the most critical fighting skill you must enhance is your speed and explosiveness. It is likely that a vampire will approach you unseen in a blitzing attack. You must be able to act quickly in response to your opponent's initial assault, defend your vulnerabilities, and launch your own counterattack.

Wheelchair-Bound Combatants—Chair-bound combatants' greatest vulnerability in a vampire assault is clearly their limited mobility. A healthy, able-bodied human will be challenged in outmaneuvering his undead attacker; imagine the difficulty faced by an individual restricted by the constraints of a wheelchair. As with all disabled combatants, however, this disability can also afford an advantage in vampire combat, provided the individual prepares in advance.

While in one respect the chair acts as a limitation, it can also be your greatest asset against an advancing ghoul. Unlike non-disabled vampire combatants who must hide their weapons awkwardly in their clothing or affix them directly to their body, as a wheelchair-bound combatant, you can stash a veritable undead arsenal in a variety of easy-to-reach locations on the apparatus itself. Within the armrests, on the seat underside, and along the backrest, the chair can become not only your means of mobility but also your arms depot.

While other types of disabled combatants may still be able to momentarily evade an attacking vampire, as a wheelchair-bound combatant, you should face the reality that there is little to no chance you will be able to outmaneuver your bloodsucking opponent. It is imperative that at the moment you realize a vampire combat engagement is inevitable, you prepare yourself for the attack rather than look for a means of escape. This means not only readying a weapon, but also positioning your body so that your opponent has limited angles at which it can initiate its assault. Fortunately, many of the techniques featured earlier work just as effectively for disabled combatants as they do for able-bodied fighters. Wheelchair-bound warriors also have the added advantage of stronger upper bodies due to the musculature required to propel themselves forward on a daily basis. Use this strength to your advantage and endeavor to end the battle swiftly; just as with any typical human combatant, the longer the disabled fighter remains engaged with a vampiric attacker, the less likely the individual is to survive.

V. COMBAT STRATEGIES AND TECHNIQUES

Psychological Defense

One additional point needs to be emphasized for disabled combatants when it comes to a vampire's assault. As noted earlier, a vampire's attack may be not only physical in nature, but psychological as well. In order to avoid a combat engagement altogether, a vampire may attempt to use a nonthreatening strategy, particularly if the undead attacker feels that, for whatever reason, it may not prevail in a physical engagement. This strategy is generally comprised of convincing disabled victims that their existence as a vampire would be an improvement on their human way of life. This strategy relies on humans' misunderstanding that once converted to a member of the undead, the physical limitations of a disabled victim will be miraculously healed, with the individual regaining full functionality over any of their previous disabilities. As a disabled combatant, it is critical that you ignore this disinformation.

Evidence suggests that disabled humans who are attacked and are subsequently converted into vampires do not regain functionality in any limbs or organs that were disabled in their human life. While it remains to be seen if certain illnesses that affect humans do not affect vampires in the same way, blindness, deafness, and all other forms of disability are retained in the conversion process. Even if it were the case that disabilities could be healed by the conversion process, the human combatant must implicitly trust the vampiric attacker that it will convert rather than feed upon and subsequently discard his body. Trust is a virtue that cannot be afforded to this species. A vampire's intentions are not based on altruism, kindness, or generosity; they are based on selfishness, greed, and hunger.

PROTECTING CHILDREN FROM VAMPIRE ATTACK

In the wild, it is often the case that the most susceptible targets are also the youngest and weakest members of the pack. This is also the case in the predatory environment between vampires and their human prey. Children's small stature, lack of strength, and general level of innocence often make them the ideal target for a vampire's evening hunt. Additionally, children are often targeted by creatures of the night for other, more nefarious reasons, which we shall explore further in this section. Not only is it recommended that you discuss the threat of a vampire attack with your children, it is your duty as a parent and the guardian of your family to arm them with the knowledge that can enable them to survive.

When discussing optimal ways to protect your loved ones from the clutches of the undead, you should adjust your strategy and communication depending on the age of the child under your protection. As with many aspects of child-rearing, defending your offspring against a vampire assault grows more difficult as they age. Thus, we will divide our discussion into several age-appropriate categories:

Infants (0–2 years)

For obvious reasons, children of this age range are clearly the most vulnerable, and are completely reliant upon you for the most rudimentary survival tasks. On the other hand, they are also the most easily protected from a vampire assault. During these early years of life, infants are rarely away from a parent's side, and are often asleep before night has fallen. Although they are completely helpless, infants can for the most part be effectively insulated from a vampire's clutches with minimal effort. Given their size and blood volume, they also are rarely targets for the undead.

Recommended Tactics: There are several specific tactics worth noting for protecting infants under your care. Should you find yourself and your child outdoors when the sun sets, endeavor to complete your journey in an enclosed structure, such as a carriage or vehicle, or make your way to a heavily traveled area, such as an open market, tourist attraction, or shopping mall. Your chances of being targeted by a bloodthirsty ghoul in a high-traffic location are slim, so ensure that you are one among many, and never, ever isolated with your child.

At this age, you may also present your child with decorative items that can aid in their own protection despite their defenseless nature. In many cultures, it is tradition to present gifts of silver to young infants in order to ward off evil spirits. In Cambodia, parents would decorate their children's ankles

with silver bracelets adorned with chiming bells, not only to drive away evil, but to monitor their children's proximity. While this may seem like a sentimental old-wives' tale, historical sources of this tradition are rooted in protecting children from precisely the type of threat that is the focus of this text. A plain silver necklace or bracelet, innocuous to the untrained eye, can serve as a simple defensive measure against the undead.

Toddlers (2–5 years)

Although children at this age begin to grow in independence from their parents, they are still heavily reliant upon them for many of their day-to-day tasks. Like infants, they are also often asleep before the sun has set—a significant safety advantage. Some children may have a natural fear of the dark and monsters—both beneficial traits in guarding them from a bloodthirsty ghoul. However, toddlers also begin to interact more frequently with other children, building their socializing abilities through playtime activity. Thus, it is at this time when your children will recognize other youngsters as playmates. This is the reason why the education of your offspring on the threat of the undead must begin at this age.

Recommended Tactics: While you want to avoid instilling an unnecessary sense of fear or dread, it is valuable to introduce basic tenets of protection in your children's fresh, receptive minds at this age. Reminding them not to venture far beyond your view, to avoid speaking to strangers, and not to let others into your home are all simple rules, but they have the potential to develop into the ingrained behaviors that can very well save their lives as they grow older, out of your protective sight.

V. COMBAT STRATEGIES AND TECHNIQUES

Children/Preteens (5–12 years)

It is during this stage of a child's life when vulnerability to the undead begins to increase dramatically from the early years. Not only are children beginning to develop into young adults, yearning for independence from the watchful eyes of their parents; many activities will center on locations outside the home, often concluding after nightfall. Extracurriculars, sporting events, and sleepovers are examples of events where your children will be outside of your protective sphere. It is also during these years when media exposure can exert a heavy influence on their as-yet-undefined personalities. There are thousands of books, films, and television programs available that contain inaccurate vampire lore, which may have an undue persuasion on your child's perception of this very real threat.

It is at this age when you should also begin to enforce the rule with your children that others are not allowed to be invited over for play without prior parental approval. While it is rare that children at this age will encounter a vampire in their normal routine, it sets the stage for when they are older, when the risk of invitation becomes much more detrimental to the entire family unit.

Recommended Tactics: If you have begun the training process earlier in your children's lives, then they will already be knowledgeable enough to avoid precarious situations that may leave them open and vulnerable. Ensure that any activities that involve being outside after sunset are monitored closely by other adults, and never allow them to travel home alone on foot. Children of this age tend to travel in larger packs for the camaraderie of their peers, which is also beneficial to their safety.

While heavily censoring the reading and viewing material is not encouraged, be mindful of what your children are absorbing related to the vampire mythos. It is during these years that children formulate the romanticized vision of the vampiric creature, a perception that may stay with them for the remainder of their lives and leave them susceptible to a ghoul's advances. Should your children consume material of this nature, be sure to remind them that the portrayal they are seeing is imprecise. Depending on the age of the child, it may be advisable to present them with this text as an alternative, accurate viewpoint.

Another threat you should be aware of is less pervasive, but warrants mentioning. Humans can be turned into the undead at any point in their lives, including childhood. In addition to the different vampire sects discussed earlier, there is another, less prominent subset of ghoul class: vampiric children. These particular creatures focus on the vulnerability and open, inviting nature of youth to accomplish their feeding objectives. As they themselves have the outward appearance of a child, the threat perceived by another child or adult is almost nonexistent, exactly the creature's intention. Often they will target the bedroom windows of their victims, hoping their appearance and powers of persuasion will gain them entrance into the home, where they will wreak havoc on the entire household. Remind your child to be wary of all strangers, whether a child or an adult, especially after nightfall, and to never invite others into the home, regardless of their appearance, age, or persuasiveness.

Teenagers (13–17 years)

The defiant years of a teenager are fraught with anxiety for a parent, independent of the vampire threat. It is during this age when children seem to instinctively contradict, argue, and defy any previous rules you have set forth for them. Teenagers also spend more and more of their time outside of their home, and at later hours of the night. It is for these reasons that these years can be the most difficult for parents in terms of ensuring safety from a vampiric assault. Another sad truth is that teen victims often are the willing participants of a vampire's advances.

These years are also taxing on parents for protecting not just the individual child, but the entire family. Teens often invite others over to their homes unbeknownst to the parents. Should this occur with a member of the undead, the household is in severe jeopardy. Whole families have been annihilated due to the naïve invitation by a teenage member of the home. You not only must stay aware of your child's friends and whereabouts, but advise them that under no circumstances should they invite strangers into the home without first being granted permission, even for the most innocuous of reasons.

Recommended Tactics: The most important tactic to secure the safety of your child at this trying age is not to have waited to discuss it with them in the first place. At this point, you've hopefully had more than a decade of influence to ensure your child makes the right decisions when outside your purview, under the vulnerable night sky. As we detailed in the recommendations for preteens, you must keep an eye on the types of media consumed by your teen. Most of the vampire subject matter popular with teenagers will have the distorted view of the creature as "the misunderstood outcast," a character heavily identified with teenagers at this awkward stage of life. It is crucial that you provide the voice of clarity to your child. While your child's perception may be that a vampire seeks understanding and affection, tell them the truth: All it wants is their blood.

At this age, you may also consider arming your child appropriately. While we do not recommend providing your offspring with a cache of weapons, you may want to consider supplying them with some defensive items: A vial of garlic mace, a silver neck chain, or a compact stake can provide a modicum of safety. It is also advised that you begin an active conditioning and combat training program for your children, if you have not already started one. Use the exercises and techniques described earlier to form the basis of a vigorous undead defense program for all your offspring, regardless of gender. Do not believe the misguided notion that daughters are more at risk. In the eyes of the undead, we are all equally vulnerable.

CONFRONTING MULTIPLE ATTACKERS

Facing off with a single member of the undead is demanding enough; imagine the difficulty in confronting multiple vampires simultaneously. Due to the physical superiority of the creature, battling a single bloodsucker can drain even the fittest of human combatants; multiply your opponents by a factor of two or three, and you have a situation that leaves you little room for error. Much as in unarmed vampire combat, there is a strong likelihood that you may not survive when confronted alone by multiple vampire attackers.

All hope, however, is not lost. Should you find yourself in the extremely precarious situation of confronting multiple vampires, use the following strategies to help you survive to see another sunrise.

Avoid the Envelope—What often occurs in a multiple-attacker engagement is that your adversaries will attempt to "close the envelope," or execute a flanking maneuver trapping you

between attackers with no hope of escape. It is vital to keep moving during your engagement, and avoid being stationary for any length of time. Due to their agility, vampires can execute a flanking attack before the human even recognizes what is happening. You must keep your body active and mobile at all times.

Do the Minimum—Your primary goal when confronted by more than a single vampire is *not* to neutralize your attacker. While there are skilled combatants who can dispatch an opponent before the other attackers converge, most individuals will not have such combat proficiency. What often occurs in multicombatant scenarios is that while you are delivering your finishing blow to one opponent, the remaining ones will use that opportunity to launch their offensive, sacrificing their companion for the sake of the hunt. It may sound counterintuitive, but your objective should be to address each threat with the minimum amount of force required for you to make your escape. Being obsessive about neutralizing a single vampire may cause you to spend an inordinate amount of time with one contender, leaving you open to the remaining attackers.

Load Your Hands—Complementing the recommendations above, you should arm yourself appropriately for a multiple attacker engagement. While a stake may be the best weapon in a one-on-one encounter, there are other possibilities once multiple opponents come into play. Against a group of vampires, your armaments need to be able to do just enough damage to allow for your escape. A long-bladed weapon is preferable, but not particularly easy to conceal or transport in the open. One option available to you is the "fist-loading" technique. Taking advantage of a vampire's vulnerability to garlic and/or silver, you can cover your fists in materials laced with these elements. This is the rare instance where conventional punches may be useful in a vampire attack; a hand wrapped in a fine silver necklace can become an effective temporary deterrent against an oncoming vampire. As one of your opponents draws close, attack it with your loaded fists. Several strikes to the visage of an attacking vampire can cause enough temporary damage to reduce its ability to counterattack. You are then free to address the other opponents until you can escape or your opponents make a hasty retreat. Once a member of the attacking party is incapacitated, the others may decide to call off the offensive and pursue alternative prey, seeing that their choice of victim is not as easily conquered as originally thought.

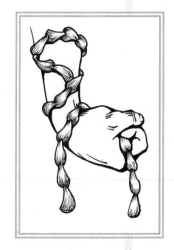

As difficult as a multiple-attacker situation is, you can rest easier in the knowledge that it is also an infrequent occurrence. Although vampires may reside with other members of their species in a single nest, they do not frequently exhibit a pack-hunting strategy, with the majority

V. COMBAT STRATEGIES AND TECHNIQUES

preferring to hunt solo. The reasoning for this is fairly simple, and indicative of the general personality of the creature. Pack hunters must share their prey with other members, and the divvying up of a single victim's blood is not the preferred choice for the species. Unless bringing down an especially large endocombatant victim, a vampire would much rather hunt alone and risk an unsuccessful feeding than have to share its prey with other succubi. Such is the egotism and selfishness of this creature.

Let us address another myth that has been perpetrated in regard to confronting multiple undead creatures: that destruction of some type of commander, figurehead, or "head vampire" will somehow cause the cycle of contagion to be broken, freeing those subjects turned by said leader and returning them to the world of the living. If this were indeed the case, it would be much simpler to reduce or eliminate the vampire threat by focusing all extermination efforts on this solitary being. Unfortunately, this is yet another vampire misconception. Each individual succubus is its own singular entity, with no connection, bond, or supernatural union to any other, including its original conversion host. There is no hierarchical chain reaction created when destroying any single vampire. This is what makes the undead threat so difficult to address—for every creature neutralized, dozens more may be created by already existing converts. It is a war of attrition that, left unchecked, may be a conflict where humanity does not emerge victorious.

COMBAT DRILLS

An axiom often said by warriors preparing for combat is: "Train hard; fight easy." Nowhere is this saying truer than in vampire combat. The harder you prepare for such an engagement in your training sessions, the better you will fare when facing an actual member of the undead. Beyond physical conditioning and techniques, one of the best ways to prepare for an undead engagement is the use of specific combat drills and simulations.

Different from conditioning and technique training, combat drilling acclimates your body to specific battle scenarios and can also help boost your confidence level through repetition. Combat drills are also designed to place you in an unorthodox and uncomfortable position, modeling a situation that may occur during an actual vampire engagement, but in a safe environment.

As these drills are used to simulate actual vampire combat, you will need the use of a training partner who is willing to play the adversarial undead role. Do not take partner selection lightly, as it will largely dictate the success or failure of your drilling sessions. Be certain to choose a partner who views vampire combat training as seriously as you do. At the same time, be clear at the outset of the exercise on what level of exertion at which the drill should be conducted; an overzealous training partner may end up injuring you in the process, which will hinder your training and leave you even more vulnerable than if you had not trained at all.

As with any sparring session, start slowly and carefully when attempting these drills for the first time, and operate at 25 percent of your maximum speed and power. As you and your partner grow adept at the various scenarios, increase your physical variables gradually until you are operating at full speed.

- **Standing to Staking**—This is the most basic of vampire combat drills, where one combatant portrays the human and the other simulates the bloodsucker. With both partners starting in a standing position, each combatant has a specific goal during the exercise: biting or staking. Obviously, the staking will be simulated in the drill's context, but the objective here is to conduct a dynamic sparring session where movements are unpredictable and reactions can be tested. If the training vampire can secure a simulated hold or bite on the neck or one of the limbs for more than ten seconds, it should be assumed that the vampire is triumphant. Conduct this drill for five minutes, monitoring how many times each partner is either staked or fed on. While you can run the drill for a longer duration, it is recommended that you do not extend it beyond a ten-minute period. Most vampire engagements last only a few minutes, so it is worthwhile to learn how to engage, counterattack, and neutralize a vampire in as short a time as possible.

- **Blindman's Bluff**—There is no question that in a vampire engagement, you will be operating in near complete darkness. Not only must a vampire feed during nocturnal hours; it often utilizes the cover of night to its advantage. One method of preparing for an attack in a low-light environment is by drilling the "blindman's bluff." The goal of this drill is to keep your training partner from securing a biting hold on you by utilizing all your other senses, as well as developing your physical reactions and sensitivity to your opponent's movements. Facing off with your training partner, cover your eyes so that your vision is completely impaired, and defend against your partner's latching attempts. Once proficient at defending the attack, you can incorporate training weapons to hone your ability to stake while blindfolded. This can be a harrowing drill to perform for those not used to operating without the use of their eyes, which is why it is essential that such a drill be practiced before encountering a vampire in a similar situation.

- **Handicapping**—Fending off a voracious vampire is traumatic enough; imagine having to do so without the use of a limb. In fact, this can be a very common scenario should an attacking ghoul catch you unaware and incapacitate one of your appendages before you are able to launch your offensive. Rather than fear such a situation, anticipate it by conducting a handicapping drill. Face off against your partner as you would in the standing to staking drill, except without the use of a particular limb. When first running this exercise, you can determine beforehand which appendage will be incapacitated for the duration of the session. As you become a more skilled combatant, have your partner call out the immobilized limb (left arm, right leg, et cetera) as you commence the session. Being able to attack and neutralize a vampire without the use of multiple limbs is difficult, but not impossible, especially if you have drilled for the scenario in anticipation of this challenging event.

VI.

TEAM-BASED COMBAT

Non Habebis Meum Sanguinem.

— UNKNOWN

In the introduction of this text, we stated that the information divulged throughout this work should not be construed as a "vampire hunter's guide." Beyond the reasoning previously made for this distinction, there is the inherent meaning to the word "hunt." Hunting has been performed by cultures around the world for one of two purposes: for sport or for food. Neither of these purposes has relevancy when engaging a member of the undead in combat. Some may consider this a semantic point, but we must not make light of the seriousness of engaging with this creature; nor should we take an air of superiority, even after extensive vampire combat training. It is precisely when we underestimate our opponent that we will fall victim to its lethal embrace.

We recognize, however, the fact that there may be circumstances when you will need to seek out and destroy a vampire in your midst. Perhaps a creature is conducting relentless incursions on your town or city. Perhaps it is targeting your family. Whatever the reason, should you need to proactively locate and exterminate a vampire with extreme prejudice, the best method to do so would be to recruit a team of individuals to assist you in your task. With several individuals acting as one against a single vampire, there is an excellent chance for a successful outcome.

TEAM ASSEMBLY

It is without question that proactive vampire extermination should be a team-based effort. The only reason to engage in one-on-one combat with a vampire is if you have no other choice. As you are targeting a vampire for termination, it is in your best interests to do so with several trusted and skilled operators who can provide support and assistance.

How many combatants will you require? While any number greater than one is beneficial, a team of three or four operators can work quite effectively, each member being tasked with a specific objective. Although having a great number of operators can help accomplish your objective more efficiently, a much larger team should be divided into smaller tactical groups, with each group operating as a single, cohesive unit and each member assigned a specific role.

Team Skill Set

A chain is only as strong as its weakest link. Nowhere is this axiom more valid than in your vampire extermination team, or e-team. While each combatant will have a separate role to perform based on his or her specific expertise, every member should possess an equivalent set of basic proficiencies:

- **Fitness Level**—Each member of your team should be in superior physical condition. Use the exercise regimen detailed in the chapter on physical conditioning to determine how prepared each member of your team will be in your excursion. Being an Olympic-caliber athlete is not required, but keep in mind that a poorly conditioned combatant can put the entire team at risk.

- **Combat Aptitude**—Every member of your team should be well versed in vampire anatomy as well as the proper combat techniques to neutralize your opponent should contact be made with the creature. While not every member may have a role in terminating the vampire, every member should be properly armed should the situation require it.

> - **Casualty Care**—One member of your team should be
>   equipped to administer advanced medical services
>   should another of your team become severely injured.
>   However, every combatant should be able to treat
>   minor wounds incurred in the heat of battle. Ideally,
>   each member of your team should be certified in
>   cardiopulmonary resuscitation and basic first aid.

Team Roles

As in any effective organization, each member of your e-team
should have a specific function in your mission. While it may
seem indulgent and unnecessary at first glance, providing
roles to each combatant clarifies the required tasks of every
member and avoids team confusion in the heat of battle.
Depending on the size of your group, each member can perform one specific role or serve several different capacities in
pursuit of your singular objective: extermination of your undead enemy.

The Medic

Much like a combat physician, this member of your team will
have the vital responsibility of tending to any severe wounds
inflicted by your attackers. Having an actual emergency room
physician in this role is ideal, but certainly not required.
Emergency medical technicians and registered nurses also
have the skills necessary to perform well in this role, as do
those with battlefield medical experience. The medic should
be prepared with a wider array of tools and equipment at their
disposal, the most important being items to treat wounds
often obtained in vampire combat: bone fractures and hemor-
rhaging caused by lacerations and deep-trauma bite wounds.

The Baiter

The most dangerous of the team positions, it is the responsibility of the baiter to directly engage the vampire and secure it for the other members to assist in executing a neutralizing blow. The individual who fills this role is typically the most skilled of the team members, as it will require all of this individual's knowledge and technique to survive once a vampire initiate its attack. Baiters are used more often in specific types of extermination missions that require a human to place himself in a compromising position in order to draw their adversary out into the open.

The Wrangler

The role of an e-team's wrangler is to essentially save the life of the baiter once the attacking vampire has been engaged. Much like an animal control technician will secure a wild beast, the wrangler will separate and place the vampire in a position to allow for a neutralizing strike. The individual who takes on this responsibility is usually the physically strongest on the team, as there will be several moments where the wrangler must use force to control the creature long enough to eliminate the attacker. In raiding operations, the wrangler is also commonly responsible for breaching the entrance of the vampire residence, and as such must have an appropriate tool, such as a sledgehammer or Halligan bar, among their equipment. Depending on the target, more than one wrangler can be employed in an operation. Also similar to a pest control expert, the wrangler must be skilled in the appropriate use of tools to secure its target, such as ropes, lassos, and snares. Veteran wranglers often design and customize their own equipment, incorporating elements known to be deleterious to the undead, such as garlic and fine silver, in order to facilitate their success.

The Closer

The individual most important to the successful completion of your operation, the closer is responsible for executing the coup de grace, or finishing blow, to the immobilized creature. Like the baiter, this position requires deep technical knowledge and skill, as well as a detailed understanding of vampire anatomy in order to execute a quick and efficient strike. The closer must also be a strategic individual who can assess the ideal way to deliver the neutralization depending on how the vampire is being controlled. Closers often only have a few seconds in which to complete their task; an unsuccessful closer can put themselves in danger and place the mission at risk. Given their role, closers are the most well-armed individuals on the team, as it will be their responsibility to ensure the secured creature is fully neutralized, regardless of how many strikes are required.

Team Equipment

Once your team is established, it is critical to review a list of gear you will need during an extermination operation. Based on the position, each member will have his own unique list of necessary equipment. However, the team should also create a universal list of required items to prepare for any unusual situations that may arise. Below is a basic list of necessities that every team member[6] should possess in the equipment list before embarking on an operation.

---

6 While this list represents the recommended loadout for every team operator, some individuals will be unable to be so aptly prepared with all the items on this list, given what their role entails. It is up to the individual to determine how to customize their particular gear given their own strengths, weaknesses, and role on the team.

Vampire Extermination Operation

STANDARD OPERATOR LOADOUT

- 1 Basic first aid kit
- 1 Fixed blade combat knife (unserrated)
- 1 Silver chain (fine silver)

- 1 Long-blade weapon
- 1 Molotov cocktail
- 1 Firearm (for use against human/animal aggressors)

- 3 Staking weapons (minimum)
- 10 Flex-cuffs
- 10 Cloves of garlic, peeled (per team member)

COMMUNICATION

A key aspect of a successful operation is close communication with all members of the e-team. At the same time, overt announcements are to be avoided in order to maintain as much of an element of surprise as possible. So how are you able to communicate clearly with your team while still maintaining operational silence? Through the effective use of hand and arm signals.

Body communication has been used successfully by military and law enforcement teams in operations for years. Take advantage of their expertise by familiarizing yourself with these standard signs.

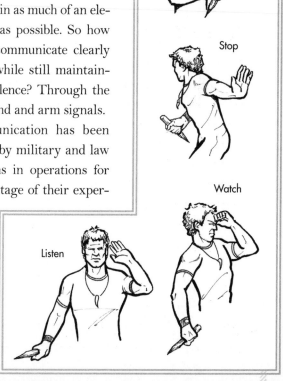

Come

Stop

Watch

Listen

VI. TEAM-BASED COMBAT

There are also a variety of signals you can utilize that are specific to vampire combat operations.

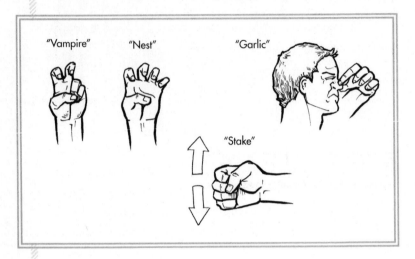

Target Confrontation

We have seen it depicted time and again in vampire-themed media: The renowned vampire slayer strolls confidently through the creature's lair. Coming upon an ominous-looking sarcophagus, he effortlessly flings off the cover to reveal a dozing bloodsucker, which he promptly stakes through the heart, hardly breaking a sweat. Mission accomplished. This scene would be comical were it not so tragically flawed. Many who believed such scenes to be fact rather than fiction have met their sad demise within a vampire's resting habitat.

A myth not previously addressed but which deserves additional clarification relates exactly to the scene described above. While their portrayal in media would have you believe that vampires are completely comatose during their daily restorative sessions, the truth is that the creature is not catatonic. Even in daylight, vampires can move freely about, provided they insulate themselves from the damaging ultraviolet rays of the sun. The likelihood of you coming upon a creature in its resting place, completely prostrate and waiting to suffer your neutralizing blow, is slim. Once discovered, there is a possibility that your adversary will begin to retaliate fiercely. However, the creature may be in a semi-dozing and lethargic state due to a recent feeding. It is for this reason that timing your operation to coincide with the vampire's most vulnerable hours is crucial. During its recuperative period, the superior physical abilities exhibited by the creature dissipate considerably once the sun rises again. While formal physiological measurements have not been taken, it is safe to say that the battlefield is far more level during a daytime operation. It is for this reason that although vampire operations are extremely hazardous, their success rate increases significantly should your team actually be able to locate the creature and engage it in combat.

COMBAT REPORT: NAME UNKNOWN

Vampire
Miami, Florida

I pass through the entrance of Black Sun, the most renowned goth club in South Florida. Unlike many establishments that only schedule specific gothic-themed evenings, Black Sun caters exclusively to this particular clientele every night of the week. The entire club is packed with what could be members of the vampire Seducer sect—strikingly attractive people clad in muted shades of black. My hand goes instinctively to my pocket where I've placed

Firestone's knife—my only defense should I find myself in a threatening situation against the undead.

I make my way through the teeming dance floor toward the rear of the club, where I locate my interview subject, seated in an empty booth. In a room filled with attractive people, my subject still stands shoulders above everyone in appearance. It is stunningly handsome, and would put most cinematic leading men to shame. Besides the mesmerizing attractiveness, my subject seems to resonate with a magnetic aura, detectable even before I come in close proximity to its presence. Its gaze never diverts from me as I awkwardly maneuver my way through the crowd and arrive at its table.

I slide into the booth and make an attempt at an introduction, which it blatantly ignores. I ask if it's willing to provide a nom de guerre or its given human name. I take its silence to signify a willingness to provide neither. I start my recorder and proceed with my planned line of questioning. As you will see from the resulting transcript, I learn that my subject's beauty is matched only by its extreme narcissism, a common trait among Seducers. Although I was unable to glean much insight, the behavior of the creature itself was worth noting for this text.

Vampire Combat Manual: When were you converted?

It does not reply, even though I know that it is fully aware of the answer. From my experience as an investigator, I know that remaining quiet, even for an uncomfortably long period of time, often prompts your subject to eventually respond to your question. We sit in silence for thirty minutes, with nothing but industrial music reverberating around us. Finally, my subject begins to speak.

Name Unknown: Why don't you ask me what you really want to know? What you must be salivating to discover from us.

VCM: What would that be?
NU: How did we do it? How did we make our existence, one

that was feared, revolted, and disgusted for centuries throughout the civilized world, into one that was admired and fantasized about by nearly every member of the human race in just fifty years?

Well, it certainly wasn't an easy task. For decades, the impression most people had of our species, besides their own folklore, were the images created by that damned Stoker and that hack Murnau. The sixties were a slight improvement, with the advent of the sexual revolution and changes in social norms, but most of us still had to feed using rustic methods: running down our prey like some common, flea-bitten animal. Disgusting really, and so primitive. Then, a few of our kind came up with a brilliant concept: What if we could take the sexual subtext of our feeding methods and leverage your own entertainment mediums to alter the perception of our existence? From that concept came the books, the music, the films, all delivering the same message: It is glorious to be one of us. Our orchestrated efforts over the last fifty years have paid off handsomely. It hardly requires any effort now for me to find a willing blood source. On the opening weekend of certain movies, I can feed upon mewling preteens all night. Look around you. There isn't a single human in this entire room, male or female, who wouldn't willingly open an artery should I ask, as long as I promise them entry.

VCM: Do you provide it?

NU: Please. Do you honestly believe I would risk all the work we've done by converting some hideous, depressing bloodbags? Many who think they belong among us are nothing more than glorified feeding troughs. Now that the perception of our kind has changed, our primary objective is to develop our species with the proper type of converts—those that can strengthen the mystique we've crafted. Despite what you may believe, this is not a simple process. First and foremost, the physical qualifications must be met. Just as important, though, is our psychological evaluation. All prospects are observed to ensure that once turned, the convert will be an enthusiastic and active recruit. Evaluations take time for some of us, but they come easy to me. I can break down most individuals after only a few minutes of observation.

To emphasize the point, it stares at me intensely for several seconds, its eyes scanning me up and down.

NU: From the wrinkles and looseness of flesh around your neck, I'd gather that you were once fat, but lost the weight at some point during your adolescence—not early enough in your life for your psyche to not have been damaged. You were ridiculed for your girth, and are still quite insecure about your appearance, judging by the way you hunch in your seat and your ill-fitting, billowy shirt, as if you're trying to hide your body from critical eyes. You have no small amount of body dysmorphia, and probably still consider yourself obese. As you came through the crowd toward me, you went out of your way not to jostle others despite the crowded environment. You are probably a middle child, very accommodating of others and someone who tries at all costs to avoid conflict, but you fear that this makes you appear weak.

The evaluation is distressingly accurate. I try not to acknowledge the precision of its assessment, but my subject smiles broadly nonetheless. It inhales deeply through his nostrils.

NU: Ah, that scent. How I've missed it. That is the downside of feeding upon the overtly willing; you don't trigger the same release of pheromones from your prey as you do on a hunt. There is nothing more intoxicating than the smell of fear. There was a time where I would intentionally avoid feeding upon my willing prey in order to experience that aroma. As you have probably realized, we choose not to hunt like others of our kind. Using brute force to overwhelm a target is easy. It's barbaric, making us no better than the cursed animals we were once considered. For us, it is much more satisfying to use intelligent methods to conquer our prey.

The key is finding the ideal environment. These dance halls are an obvious choice, but one of my personal favorites is your houses of worship. Humans find so much solace in these synthetic shelters, lulling you into a deliciously false sense of security. Not to mention that many still believe that someone such as myself would immediately burst into flame should I set foot in these structures. How laughable. I am able to pass through the narthex like anyone else, stride up to the lectern, and begin reading from scripture without a single lightning bolt emerging from the sky.

There was this one instance I still remember fondly. I met this female one evening at a religious studies group. She was a single mother of three, having lost her husband overseas in one of your silly wars. I imagine she hoped to meet a new mate at one of these gatherings. Instead, she met me. After only a weeks' time, she invited me into her home for dinner and to meet her children. After being invited in, I opened the door to several of my companions as well. Oh, and how we did feast. The aromas they released before we fed were divine.

You have children as well, do you not?

I remain silent, believing that this is another attempt to draw out personal information or manipulate my emotions.

NU: Two males. Logan and Jonas?

I feel the blood drain from my face. It knows the names of my children, despite my never having provided this information to any sources. I unprofessionally lose my composure and leap at my subject, gripping it around the collar. It smiles and flares its nostrils again.

NU: Now there's another smell I miss. The smell of rage. It's so rare that I encounter it any more.

Do you really believe it is your pathetic investigative skills that have enabled you to meet with the likes of us? Here's a truth you can take back to your betters—it is only due to our good graces that you are able to walk the streets at night without your head ending up on a pike, along with the rest of your family. And this war between species that you're writing? You are no more at war with us than lambs are at war with slaughterhouses. As far as your defenses against us are concerned, that pigsticker in your pocket won't help you one bit.

You keep at it, though; it has been entertaining for us. Now, I suggest you release your grip before . . .

Its thought is interrupted by a woman who crosses in front of our table. She is its equal in beauty—flawless skin, athletic build, and golden blond hair, except for a dramatic streak of red running through it. She turns slightly to meet its eyes, and then turns away. It turns its head to follow her stride. It is then I notice the scar running underneath the left ear.

I release my hands and it leaves the table without another word, in pursuit of what it believes will be its next victim.

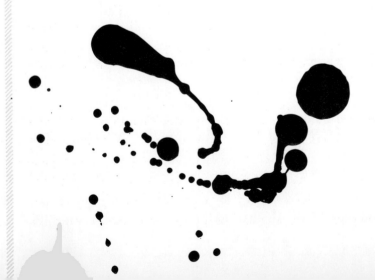

EXTERMINATION OPERATIONS

Having established your team and equipped them properly, the final step is orchestrating the operational plan. When it comes to vampire extermination, there are several ways to execute your operation. Each has its own strengths and weaknesses, and depending on various external factors such as timing, location, and team experience, you may choose one type over the other. Evaluate the following operation types and choose your method appropriately.

Stakeouts

Much like the law enforcement activity that bears the same name, stakeouts, also known as surveillance or "shadowing," are mostly utilized to track the patterns of a particular undead target in order to determine the optimal moment to initiate an assault. While many similarities exist between watching a human and surveilling a vampire, there are some pointed differences as well. Monitoring the movements of your target should be an essential component of any assault, as they will reveal not only when your opponent is most accessible, but also if the situation poses too much of a risk to your team or innocent bystanders. While effective target tracking can be a complicated endeavor, there are some simple recommendations you can follow to make your stakeout a successful one.

Maintain Distance—The most common mistake of most novice trackers is staying too close to the target. Your ultimate goal is not to hover over your mark, but to evaluate its general movements to discern if patterns exist in its nocturnal activities. Never forget that you are also dealing with a cunning adversary who may be able to detect the fact that it is being watched. Luckily, most vampires do not believe themselves to be targets during their hunting activity. Use this arrogance to your advantage.

Record Activity—An essential component of a good stakeout is detailed record keeping. As you track your target, be sure to note the smallest details—the time of the evening, the target's attire, the streets taken, the number of steps required to cross the street. No detail should be disregarded, as a seemingly insignificant piece of information may assist in your assault. Should you have the luxury of a larger team, split the monitoring of your target into shifts and locations, so that the responsibility of recording the target's activity can be borne by the entire team.

A key trait of any successful tracker is patience. Be certain to take as long as it is required to capture all the necessary information; it may take several weeks to develop a complete pattern analysis without any informational gaps for a single mark, as it is often the case that a vampire will vary its activity precisely so that its movements appear random and irregular.

Plot Strategy—Once satisfied that you have a complete picture of the creature's movements, develop an appropriate strategy based on an analysis of your data. Note the areas where your target seems to be alone and isolated. There are many external variables that can also affect the success of your operation. When plotting the details, do not overlook elements such as weather, time, and the presence of bystanders in the vicinity.

Stings

Also similar to law enforcement operations, stings entail luring the target into a setting so that the mission can be completed. In these particular situations, however, the goal is not incarceration, but annihilation of the target. While vampire stings are difficult to execute, they can be more successful than the other types of exterminations due to the fact that the creature is willingly lured into a situation orchestrated by the operations team, rather than an open assault or a raid on a vampire's lair. It is without question, however, that the success or failure of a sting largely depends on the team member interacting with the vampire itself, otherwise known as the "lamb."

Despite the delicate-sounding name, the individual in the role of the lamb is often the most experienced, skilled, and deadly member of a sting operation. The role of the lamb is, at its most basic, the same as the role of baiter. However, there are some significant differences in skill level and sophistication necessary for this covert role. Not only must this person be a proficient vampire combatant, he must be strategic, cunning, and quick-witted. Lambs mostly operate without any defensive equipment or weaponry, lest they tip their hand to the target in question. Similar to the stressful job of an undercover agent, the lamb must be able to convince the target that his manner is unassuming, his behavior innocent, and his intentions genuine. Both men and women can be equally proficient in the role of a lamb, but the success rate does seem to increase if the target and team member are of the opposite gender.

Just as there are specific recommendations for a stakeout operation, executing a sting requires its own set of unique strategies for success.

> **Eyes on Target**—The most important rule to obey during a sting operation is that at least one team member other than the lamb needs to maintain visual contact of the target at all times. The lamb will be much too preoccupied with performing the role to worry whether the rest of the team is keeping

account of the situation. Never disobey this rule; your teammate's life depends on it.

Establish a Rescue Signal—Although visual contact should be maintained at all times, the team may not be privy to exactly what is transpiring between the lamb and the target during their interaction. Should a situation develop where the lamb fears his life is in jeopardy thinks the vampire senses something un-usual, he must have a way to signal the rest of the team to either abort the operation or breach the en-gagement to rescue their teammate. Depending on the team's proximity to the target, the signal can be an audible cue, such as a word or a phrase, or a seem-ingly innocuous visual cue such as a scratching of the head, a flip of the hair, or a wiping of the brow.

Raids

Rather than facing your opponent in open territory during a stakeout operation or luring it to a specific location in a sting, raids take place in one of the most perilous of locations: the vampire's own lair. Of all the operation types, this is without question the most difficult to execute successfully and the most hazardous for team operators. Because you are facing your opponent on its own territory, there are many chances for you to fall victim to its clutches.

On the other hand, executing a raid at the vampire's abode also enables you to launch an attack when your opponent is at its weakest, rather than when its strength is at its peak. It also affords you the opportunity to ensure that the creature's resources are thoroughly destroyed, along with any other members of the species taking refuge in the same location. Because of the complexity of this type of operation, we will spend the most time covering details and providing recommendations to consider in planning a successful vampire raid.

Timing Your Raid

At this point in the text, you should be well aware of a vampire's biorhythmic cycle that enables it to operate at peak strength during nocturnal hours. As we also noted, the strength begins to wane as dawn approaches, at which time the creature must retreat to its resting place for the duration of the daylight hours. Although many military and law enforcement raids occur in the twilight or early-morning hours to take advantage of the cover of darkness and the lethargy of human targets, a vampire raid must occur when sunlight is at its peak. Thus, the optimal time to execute a raid on a vampire structure is around astronomical noon, the time of day during which the sun is at its apex in the sky. While it is not essential that any vampire engagement occur at precisely this hour, keep in mind that the further you drift from this specific time slot, the less exposed your opponent will be.

Planning Your Raid

One of the most important keys to executing a successful raid, second only to the timing, is the preparation of your raiding plan. A scene commonly depicted on film and familiar to many is the image of an operator team maneuvering into position and smoothly executing a raid on an adversary's domicile. What is not often depicted is the tedious, lengthy planning of said operation. This is no different when your target is a blood-feasting ghoul. For your own safety and that of your entire team, spend a proper amount of time preparing so

VI. TEAM-BASED COMBAT

that all tasks become second nature during the raiding campaign.

No detail is too minute when planning a raid on a vampire dwelling. Here are some of the critical elements that need to be addressed in your planning sessions.

The Floor Plan—All possible means should be utilized to secure an accurate floor plan of the target's residence prior to an operation. If you cannot located an official design plan, use other residences in the area as reference points; homes in the same neighborhood often exhibit similar layouts, especially if built by the same contracting company. Likewise, apartments often have identical floor plans running above and below the target apartment throughout the same building.

The Breach—Once a floor plan has been acquired, your team must determine how to enter the vampire residence, otherwise known as the "breach." It is advisable to breach the dwelling via nontraditional entryways, as the standard entrances are typically well monitored as well as possibly booby-trapped. Depending on the size of your team, keep the number of simultaneous breaching entries to a minimum. While you may be able to cover more ground with your teams divided, there is also more likelihood for confusion and chaos.

The Rehearsal—The most critical aspect of planning your raid is the rehearsal of the actual operation. Much like an orchestra that must practice a composition before it is perfected, cleanly executed raiding operations require a detailed rehearsal process. Rehearsals can begin as a tabletop exercise, with the assault depicted on paper or using small scale models. As each team member learns his role in the assault, rehearsals should ideally be conducted either in the similar location of the attack or in a rehearsal space that can replicate the area down to the fine details. From the number of windows and steps to each doorway to the individual responsible for clearing each room, every member of your team should be confident in his or her role during your raid. Part of your rehearsal time should also be devoted to worst-case scenario contingencies, such as the wounding of a teammate, in order to maximize the preparedness of each operator. A proper rehearsal ensures that, come raid time, your team moves instinctively, acts fluidly, and performs flawlessly.

Evaluating Raiding Structures

Ask everyday citizens what they picture when you mention a vampire's dwelling, and the image of a gothic castle rising from fog-laden moors probably comes to mind. The fact of the matter is that vampires nest in many different types of residences, both modern and archaic. The residence itself matters less to the creature than does the surrounding area. A vampire will take refuge in any number of locations, as long as it provides sanctuary from the daylight, a steady supply of nourishment, and a place to recuperate from the evening's hunt.

Once a vampire dwelling has been confirmed, you may for a moment consider destroying the entire structure via a long-distance weapon, such as fire or explosives, rather than seeking out the creature itself. Although this may seem like a plausible solution, it is not advised. Putting aside the fact that there may be innocent civilians harmed should you demolish the creature's alleged lair, utilizing an overtly destructive means will likely result in the flight of your target before your objective is complete. One of the first tasks a vampire completes on any of its residences is the creation of several escape routes in the event of a breach. If you use a remote weapon, it is more than likely that your target will escape unscathed before experiencing any permanent damage. Your team must sweep and clear the structure as it would any other, foot by foot and inch by inch. The only certain way to ensure proper neutralization is direct confrontation and elimination of your adversary.

Your opponent is also fully aware of its vulnerability during daylight recuperative hours. As such, it will place as many obstacles in your path as possible to avoid discovery and confrontation in the form of traps, attack animals, and perhaps even other humans. Your team should be alert to the fact that when raiding a vampire's compound, the battle begins not when you meet your opponent, but the moment you enter its premises.

Given the fact that different dwellings can dramatically affect your tactical approach, it is important that we take a moment to discuss the variety of structures that a vampire may utilize as its retreat.

Apartment Buildings—Housing complexes or condominiums are a common resting place for vampires residing in major urban areas. They are a preferred choice for city-dwelling bloodsuckers due to the relative anonymity of apartment living. The building residents also can be utilized as a quick source of feeding in emergency situations. Vampires who choose to live in structures such as these will often reside either on the ground or penthouse floors of such structures, allowing them easy entry and exit with minimal human

contact. They will reside in buildings that do not have doorman amenities, as such residences often attract undesired attention and interaction.

There are two primary difficulties encountered when launching a vampire raid in an apartment structure: target location and civilian interference. Vampires will often purchase several residences in the same building precisely to avoid tracking of its movements. In executing a raid on an apartment structure, it is vital to know the exact apartment in which your target is recuperating prior to mission launch. It will take far too much time to sweep through every residence on a particular floor in search of your opponent, not to mention the commotion such disturbances will cause the non-vampire population. An extensive surveillance of the target domicile must be conducted prior to commencing your attack to be certain that the apartment breached does in fact contain your resting adversary. You may consider sending undercover agents, or "ghosts," into the premises to conduct a prolonged reconnaissance over several days prior to mission launch.

Once undead occupation has been confirmed, raiding an apartment becomes much easier, as the size of the residence is typically much smaller than other types of dwellings and has minimal structural modifications. Apartment-clearing operations can be executed by a single raiding party of four to five skilled operators. Ensure that each room is cleared before moving on to adjoining rooms until you encounter your final target.

Houses—Freestanding homes present a set of challenges that are almost exactly opposite of those encountered in an apartment raid. Whereas your team needs to concern itself with target confirmation, civilian residents, and multiple locations in a housing complex, none of these issues is a concern when a vampire chooses to dwell in a single-family residence. However, there are other issues your team must contend with that are just as risky to your operation's success.

Confirmation of the dwelling as a vampire lair should be straightforward, provided your team spends the proper amount of time surveilling the location. Outward appearances may also provide clues to the presence of undead. Shades will be drawn and composed of material that prevents ultraviolet light from filtering in (Note: some vampires will enact a counterstrategy, and keep their shades raised in order to draw suspicion away from their lair, rising only once sundown is complete.) You may also question the neighboring population regarding suspicious activity or lack of the creature's presence, although vampires often select homes built on parcels of land far enough away from an inquiring population.

Once target confirmation is complete, the real challenge begins. Single-family homes are much larger than apartment dwellings and contain many adjoining rooms, basements, and attics, each of which will require a complete sweep by your team. Planning and rehearsal should be prioritized in a raiding mission on a vampire house.

Floor plans can sometimes be retrieved by consulting the local utility company or the county or municipality archives where the home is located (although this may require a formal permit or the services of an architect supportive of your cause). Should you be fortunate enough to have access to such documents, the time spent clearing a vampire lair can be abbreviated. However, vampires have been known to perform significant renovations to their dwellings in order to serve their unique purposes. Do not assume that if the creature's presence is not overtly conspicuous once all the rooms have been cleared that it is not present elsewhere in the home, perhaps in a customized renovation unseen by the naked eye.

A final word of advice regarding home raids—do not be fooled by external appearances or décor. Whether it's impeccably designed or visually repugnant, vampires often use the appearance of their dwelling to accomplish one of two objectives: to dissuade intruders or to entice victims. The few survivors of vampire attacks who have seen a ghoul's quarters and lived to tell the tale have described all manners of adornment and furnishings, none of which seemed to represent the creature itself. Much like a model home, the outward appearance should not influence your raiding team either positively or negatively. Regardless of what you may see, your operation's primary objective is always elimination of the target.

VI. TEAM-BASED COMBAT

Natural Structures—Although the focus has been on man-made structures, there may be a situation where a vampire utilizes a natural formation as its place of residence. Caves, rock dwellings, and natural grottos all may be utilized by a vampire as its primary resting place. While somewhat uncommon in this advanced era, there are several reasons why a creature would select such a structure in lieu of a modern residence.

- **Environment**—Should a vampire's region of activity be rural in nature, residing in a natural structure will draw much less attention than an artificial abode, and be much more difficult to locate by the local townsfolk.

- **Isolation**—By using a natural dwelling, vampires avoid undesired interaction with the human population, other than to feed. A high percentage of vampire Grotesques use natural structures as their residence for this very reason.

- **Security**—Vampires will select a natural structure that is extraordinarily difficult to access by a normal human, providing a degree of security from forces that would do it harm. Unlike artificial structures, natural dwellings also do not have an accessible floor plan that can be utilized by a raiding party in preparation for an attack.

In executing a raid on a natural structure, your team must exhibit extra caution. Not only will the terrain be extremely unfamiliar, but natural structures lend themselves well to the use of additional countermeasures to thwart your operation and terminate your team members, such as trip wires and antipersonnel devices. Approach natural structures as you would any raiding operation: slowly, carefully, and with an emphasis on operational planning.

Avoiding Trap Hazards

An obstacle that your team will likely encounter during your operation is a set of countermeasures created by the vampire to foil a raiding party's activities. These devices are often as deadly to the operators as the vampire itself; whole teams have been neutralized during an undead raid before an operator comes close to reaching the target.

Regardless of the raiding structure itself, patience and precision should be exhibited by your teammates at all times. Typical law enforcement raids can be executed in one of two ways: slowly via a "slow and deliberate" search, or quickly via a "dynamic entry." In a vampire raid, your method should always be slow and deliberate. Remember, time is relatively on your side. If you've scheduled your raid wisely, there is no reason why you cannot spend hours painstakingly sweeping through the structure in search of your target in the daylight while avoiding its deadly counterattacks.

Many of the trap hazards described below have been used throughout history not only to eliminate adversaries, but also to strike fear and dampen the morale of the victims. However, rather than traps that employ modern explosive devices and firepower, vampires tend to rely on natural devices that utilize piercing weaponry and crushing objects as the offensive weapons. While the motivation behind this has not been confirmed, one can hypothesize why the undead rely on organic traps. First, the sound of gunfire or an explosive detonation can draw additional attention from passersby who hear the resounding blast and may contact the authorities. Explosive-based traps also tend to be more complicated to construct and require specialized material. Natural trap hazards, on the other hand, are easy to create, require no special equipment, and are nearly silent even when tripped. Below are several of the more common vampire traps of which your team should be cognizant during your raid.

PUNJI STAKES Made famous during the Vietnam War, punji stakes are sharpened poles made of wood or bamboo, pointed upward from a camouflaged hole or depression in the ground. Used primarily to wound the lower extremities, punji pits rely on a misstep made by the operator, who will fall into the stake-lined crater. The stakes may be coated with a toxin to increase their lethality, requiring the raiding team to retreat immediately and tend to the wounded individual before proceeding. Frequently used in the vicinity of a natural structure lair, punji stakes are a popular deterrent used by vampires who savor the use of stakes as a weapon against their human adversary. Irony is apparently not lost on some members of the species.

Trap Countermeasure: Treading with a light and careful step can dramatically reduce the risk of falling into such an entrapment, but the use of a probing device, such as a long reed or staff, can also assist in

testing a questionable patch of earth. Be wary of areas that are covered in loose material such as dirt or leaves, as they may give way to something much more lethal.

WHIPS Another trap made popular in jungle warfare, whips are comprised of a flexible material such as wood, bamboo, or high-tensile steel to which are attached implements lethal in nature, such as stakes, razors, or blades. The material is bent backward and set in place by a trip wire. Once the wire is tripped, the material flexes back to its original state, flinging the sharpened objects at great velocity toward the victim.

Trap Countermeasure: The key to avoiding the whip trap, and any other device triggered by a trip wire, is to advance carefully when clearing the vampire abode. Do not use speed and aggression in vampire raiding operations. Against this particular opponent, advance confidently, but cautiously. Another unusual device you can use to locate hard-to-detect trip wires is Silly String. Shot from a canister, these light, airy strands have been used by the military for exactly this purpose. The strings can be shot in advance of a suspected area to detect any unseen wiring.

DOOR TRAPS In room-clearing operations, the doorway is without question the most unsafe location of any structure. In military parlance, this area is known as the "fatal funnel," where all forms of lethality channel toward this one narrow location. It is no different in a vampire raid. Whenever crossing a threshold of any sort, care must be taken that no trip wires or traps have been set, particularly if the room you are crossing into is shrouded in darkness.

Countermeasure: Be sure to utilize all the recommendations previously outlined in the other countermeasures: probes, Silly String, and cautious movement. Also, be sure to gain visibility into the room by shining a light into the darkness, scanning the entire location before entering as well as angling the beam into all corners of the doorframe. Do *not* reach your hand into the darkened space in search of the light switch. Your adversary may have anticipated this very action, and set up another trap for your extended limb.

COMBAT STRATEGIES

Having outlined the variety of roles within an e-team, we can now detail offensive tactics available given the number of operators at the ready for an extermination mission. Regardless of the experience level of the individual members, your strategy will vary depending on your numbers. Let us also provide some broad strategies for different team engagements.

Two-Person Teams

Dual combatants have an advantage over the vampire target, albeit a relatively minor one. Many creatures can manage two opponents simultaneously, often disposing of one before turning its attention to the second as its blood source. The key to a successful two-on-one engagement is utilizing the element of surprise as much as possible. Due to their arrogant nature, vampires perceive human attack as a momentary inconvenience. Take advantage of your opponent's underestimation.

In a two-person e-team, both operators must perform multiple roles in the engagement. It is recommended that you eliminate the role of wrangler, and instead focus on the baiter and closer roles. Once the baiter is fully engaged with the target to the point that the vampire's focus is entirely on its imminent feeding, an opportunity should present itself for the closer to strike. One example of a successful dual-operator strategy is the bait and switch.

The Bait and Switch

1. Baiter engages the vampire and executes the vise maneuver, locking the target in place. Baiter secures an L-frame grip, holding the target in position and focusing the creature's attention on himself.

2. Closer maneuvers into position and executes a neutralizing blow from the rear using the Assassin Stake.

Three-Person Teams

In a three-person team, you have the luxury of having one of your teammates perform the role of wrangler, which creates a less risky situation for the team's baiter. The benefit of having a wrangler during your operation is that the person who first engages the vampire need not spend as much time securing the target until the closer can move in for a finishing strike. The wrangler's objective in a three-person e-team is to extricate the vampire as quickly as possible from the baiter so that any further harm can be avoided.

The other benefit of having an active and well-equipped wrangler on your team is that direct contact with the creature can be kept at a minimum. The individual in this role needs to be skillful with a snaring device, so that the team can execute neutralizing techniques such as the rodeo.

The Rodeo

1. Baiter engages the vampire and executes the vise maneuver, forcing the head of the creature upward using the bull grip.

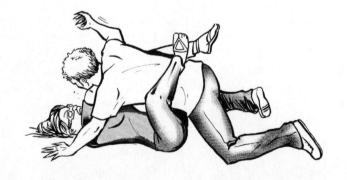

2. With the creature's head upright, the wrangler secures a hold around the neck with a restraining device and pulls the creature off the baiter.

3. The wrangler pins the vampire's head to the ground using the snare. Once secured, the baiter can assist in restraining the creature as the closer moves into position and executes a decapitating strike using a heavy-bladed weapon.

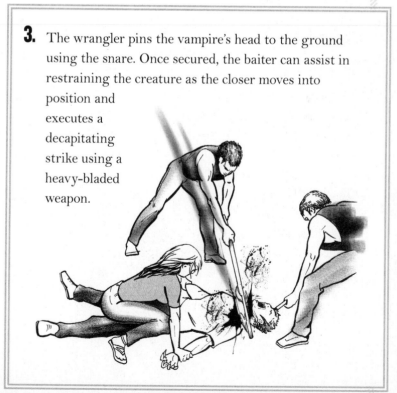

VI. TEAM-BASED COMBAT

Four-Person Teams

Quite possibly the minimum number for a single e-team, a four-person assault squad not only allows every member of your team to carry out a unique function; it affords greater security in any extermination operation. Should you not have an experienced medic available, two operators can perform the roles of wranglers, making it easier to secure your target for neutralization. Having two wranglers is also beneficial when engaging with physically stronger vampires, such as those in the Supremist class. In fact, you should operate with no fewer than four members if you know that your target is a member of that particular vampire sect.

With two wranglers both operating trapping snares, the vampire can be secured in a prone position that provides the closer with several options for his finishing blow. One excellent use of the dual-wrangler strategy is a technique called the T-Bone.

The T-Bone

1. Baiter executes the standard vise maneuver on the undead attacker. Operator then secures a grip on the cloth around each of the vampire's wrists and pulls its arms open and upward. This movement can also be done one arm at a time should the creature be too powerful.

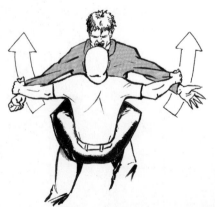

2. Wranglers position themselves on each side of the target and loop snares around each of the creature's exposed wrists.

3. Both wranglers simultaneously pull the vampire's arms backward and pin them to the ground, outstretched. Baiter lowers himself on the creature's body, exposing the chest cavity. With the thoracic cage fully exposed, the closer positions himself alongside the target for a finishing stake or decapitating blow.

VI. TEAM-BASED COMBAT

Confronting a Hive

One of the most intense combat scenarios an assault team can encounter when executing a raid on a vampire lair is exposing a "hive," a nest of vampires occupying a single dwelling. There may or may not be a relationship between the vampires who take up the same residence. This point, however, should not be of great concern to you; remember, your team's role is that of an exterminator. In situations such as this, however, your mission becomes notably more complicated.

Should your team come upon a vampire hive stealthily with none of the creatures rising to initiate a counterattack, consider yourselves lucky. What this signifies is that the creatures have recently fed, and the combination of a full belly and the natural biorhythmic weaknesses resulting from the time of day has left them susceptible to your team's attack. Should this be the case, you must operate with haste, utilizing the following recommendations to effectively address the situation.

- **Run the Numbers**—Assess how many creatures you must neutralize. If the hive size outnumbers your team by a ratio of 2:1, vampire to human, it is recommended you take the scorched earth approach (see below).

- **Move with Speed**—There's no telling at what point the hibernating vampires will become aware of the breach and rise to counterattack. Thus, the team's movements must be quick, instinctive, and without hesitation.

- **Set the Stage**—Should the number of team members equal or outnumber the quantity in the hive, each operator should arrange himself alongside one of the creatures.

- **Attack as One**—Much like a conducted orchestra, every member should launch a neutralizing strike simultaneously along with the team, so that the extermination of a single creature will not rouse the others to attack. The assault can be either a staking maneuver or a decapitation strike. While somewhat more difficult, a decapitation attack may be the preferable method against a prone, unresisting vampire.

- **Scorched Earth Approach**—Should your team find itself outnumbered by the hive, and you do not have the time or resources to retreat and call for additional support, you have the alternative of launching a scorched earth attack. Utilizing the Molotov cocktails that were recommended in your standard equipment loadout, each operator should ignite his own torch. When all cocktails are fully lit, the team should station themselves just outside the hive entrance and launch their weapons in a single coordinated firestorm into the room, targeting the creatures themselves or any materials in the nest with a high likelihood of rapid immolation. After this launch, the entrance to the hive should be blocked, and the team should position themselves outside the entranceway for any ghouls attempting to make their escape. Fleeing vampires can be struck down by the monitoring operators.

SECURING THE HOME

It has been often said that an individual's home is his proverbial castle. When it comes to defense from a vampire assault, this adage is absolutely the case. The one reassurance you have in terms of a vampire attack is that regardless of your opponent's superior physical abilities, you can find safe harbor in your own residence, given the vampire's inability to cross your threshold without expressed invitation.

Unfortunately, there may come a time when the sanctity and security of your home is breached by a bloodthirsty ghoul.

Whether it be through an inadvertent welcoming by another member of the household or a devious hoax executed by a vampire intent on gaining access, you may one day find yourself battling a member of the undead in your own residence. Although an unlikely scenario, you may want to anticipate such an event by preparing and equipping your domicile in advance. The following are some helpful recommendations should one evening you find that your home is at the mercy of an invading ghoul.

Avoid Booby Trapping

While there are some vampire security professionals who believe that you can never be too prepared, it is our belief that it is possible to oversecure the home. A common pitfall to avoid is setting anti-vampire devices in your own residence in the hopes of ensnaring or neutralizing your undead invader.

In addition to being your stronghold and your fortress, this place is also your family home. Any trip wires, foothold traps, or ordnance devices that you engineer are more likely to be tripped by an unsuspecting neighbor, pet, or family member than by an undead ghoul. Regardless of how meticulous and organized you may think you are, it is very likely that such traps will be more of a hindrance than a benefit to your survival. Rather than rigging your household with such devices, spend your time preparing the home in other ways.

Plant Your Weapons

Many vampire combatants often wonder, "What is the best counter-ghoul weapon?" Is it the decapitating long blade, the silver-laced garrote, or the simple yet efficient vampire stake? The answer is quite simple. The best weapon is the one you have in your hand during the moment of attack. This maxim

is particularly relevant when the attack is occurring inside your home. Since it is uncertain in which room the confrontation will take place, prepare for a potential breach by ensuring that a variety of weapons are stored throughout the home should you need them. These armaments should also be out of view of your adversary in order to retain the element of surprise, as well as not alarm other humans who may enter the residence.

The key to successfully planting your weapons is placing them in areas where they are easily accessible, completely out of sight, and not in the most obvious of locations. Some options for weapon concealment include:

- Undersides of tables
- Above doorway entrances
- Behind side tables and sofas
- Alongside bedframes

It is recommended that you store at least one armament per room in the domicile. Should the room be larger in dimension, such as a living room, library, or bedroom, more than one stashed weapon is advised. Be sure to place them in separate and distinct locations should one area of the room become compromised and inaccessible to you.

Seed with Garlic

Although rigging the entryways and rooms with booby-trapped trip wires is not recommended for the aforementioned reasons, you can take advantage of your adversary's unique vulnerabilities to create obstacles that will deter your assailant while being harmless to other human residents. Seeding the apertures of your home with threads of garlic can help to deter entrance through those gateways. Do not believe the myth that once invited, a vampire's vulnerabilities become null and void—this is another rumor perpetrated by the species to deter use of these items in your home.

Much like the garlands we described in the section on secondary weapons, garlic threads are inexpensive and simple to create. Using a fresh bulb of raw garlic, peel all the cloves and thread them onto a line of fishing wire. Instead of tying off the ends to create a garland, you will instead leave them open, creating a single line of raw, threaded cloves that can be strung across a windowsill or doorway. Using bunches of threaded cloves, you can create a curtain of garlic highly repulsive to an attacking vampire. The downside of using this particular deterrent is the odor it will emit throughout your home. Should the smell of raw garlic not disturb your family or your neighbors, seeding your home with them can be an effective countermeasure to the breaching vampire.

Create a Safe Room

The nightmare has become reality: Your home is breached, your family is in peril, and the invading bloodsucker is running rampant in your home. Rather than put yourself in additional jeopardy by confronting your attacker, retreat may be a better alternative. But where can you turn? The outdoors is not an option, considering the time of day; a neighbor's home is an unlikely refuge as well. In anticipation of such an event, you may want to dedicate a room in your home where you can beat a path of retreat. Not only is this a practical solution, it is one that is relatively easy to create and successful at keeping the undead at bay, provided you design it with your adversary in mind.

Creating a safe room that can protect you from vampire attack is very different from one that insulates you from human intruders. Whereas in most cases managing situations against the undead is more difficult, creating a vampire safe room is actually easier. The key will be creating an environment inhospitable to even a momentary vampire intrusion. How can you create such an environment? By taking advantage of one of the most basic vulnerabilities known to a vampire: ultraviolet light.

Whereas in the past ultraviolet lamps were unavailable to the general population and accessible only for professional and educational use, today they are readily available and reasonably priced. By bathing the room in the bright, bluish glow of several UV lamps, you ensure that your opponent will be unable to infringe on your location without suffering excruciating pain. Be certain to direct the beams so that it encompasses the entire room, and ensure that you are powering them with an independent energy source separate from the rest of your home. You can be certain that once the creature sees the predicament you have created, its first strategic move will be to cut the power to your residence.

The room itself need not be large in size—only great enough to comfortably fit yourself and any family members under your protection. In fact, it is better if the room is more compact, as it will be easier and less expensive to engulf the room completely with UV light. It is advised that you store a small weapons cache within the room, as well as bottled water. Remember, you do not need to remain enclosed in the space for days on end; only long enough for the sun to rise.

PEACEFUL COEXISTENCE

There are those who wonder, given the power and spheres of influence acquired by the vampire species, whether it is a wise decision to provide a comprehensive battle plan against such a creature as we have in this text. Would it not be a better alternative to find a way to peacefully coexist with this species, rather than provoke and antagonize such dangerous inhabitants of our society?

The fact is we have been coexisting with them for hundreds of years, living as victims often do, in blind ignorance of their threat. While it may be the case that you go through your entire life without ever having to confront a bloodsucking member of the undead, the likelihood of it never occurring grows more slim.

In the past sixty years, the world population has grown more than 100 percent, from approximately 3 billion in 1960 to 7 billion in 2012. As a comparison, it took 150 years to grow to 3 billion people from 1804 to 1960. While this extraordinary leap in the world population means a vast source of food to the vampire society, it also presents a tremendous threat. Not only do our increased numbers mean an encroachment on the habitats of the undead population; it also signifies to many in the vampire community that what humans lack in physical superiority, we could very well make up for in sheer overpowering numbers. As a result, there is a growing consensus among the undead that perhaps a time draws near when it would be better to "thin the herd." Should this decision eventually be acted upon by the vampire species, the majority of human beings will have no idea how to defend themselves or their loved ones from this intimidating adversary. You will not be one of them.

COMBAT REPORT:
PAUL LAVIN

Professor, Ancient Languages
San Francisco, California

I'm seated in the office of Paul Lavin, professor of ancient languages at San Francisco City College, waiting for him to return for our interview. As can be expected for the office of an educator, books are piled high from floor to ceiling along each of the walls. There is no evidence present, however, of Lavin's former career. Prior to his life in higher education, Paul Lavin was known as Father Lavin, a Roman Catholic priest. Lavin was one of a handful of clergy performing a specialized skill for the Church—demonic evictions, otherwise known as exorcisms.

I stand as Lavin enters the room. He moves slowly, as if his joints pain him to bend them, and looks much older than his fifty-four years. In my initial discussions with Lavin, I was told he was recently diagnosed with early-onset Alzheimer's, which is partially why he agreed to speak with me. As he sits, I note a jagged scar that runs along the crest of his forehead toward his right ear. Despite his fragile appearance, he seems to be a jovial spirit, with bright, smiling eyes. He retrieves a bottle of whiskey from the bottom drawer of his desk, and pours himself a drink. "I hope you don't mind," he says. "It's a habit I retained from my previous life. It is the end of the day, after all." He leans back in his chair and begins to tell a tale that not many living humans can: surviving an encounter with a vampire Supremist.

Paul Lavin: When people hear the word "exorcism," most immediately think of people strapped to beds, speaking in tongues, projectile vomiting. Reports of possession exploded in the seventies after the release of that particular film. The reality of an exorcist's work, however, is much more mundane. Ninety-nine-point-nine percent of the reported cases end up being an unfortunate instance of undiagnosed mental illness. Due to the rise in reports, however, the Church began quietly expanding its program to handle these types of cases. I was a result of their expansions. I was living in New York City at the time, and had the entire tristate area as my jurisdiction.

As intriguing as the work sounds, it is most similar in actuality to social work. If there is a suspected case of demonic possession, a formal request must be filed, an initial inquiry and site visit is made, and, if necessary, a formal exorcism is performed. Most cases never got as far as that final step. During the inquiry, if it was determined that the individual was mentally ill, then the state psychiatric agencies would take over. Regardless, once word spread of my new role, I noticed that people in the neighborhood started greeting me more often. It was one of the neighborhood women who asked me for help.

She approached me on the street one night as I finished shopping for the evening's groceries. Her English was as spotty as my Spanish, but I understood her enough to know she was asking for help. She had said that her cousin, a superintendent in the Bronx, was having serious trouble in his building with a particular resident, and demonic possession was suspected. She said she didn't want to make trouble for the Church, but she asked if there was something I could do to help. I promised her I would. From the sounds of her description, it seemed like another case of an individual not properly taking their medication, so rather than trouble the archdiocese about it, I decided to handle the situation myself.

The next night, my driver, Mohammed, took us into the South Bronx for the site visit. Mohammed was a Muslim and a Rajput, a member of the warrior class. As my driver for several years, he always made sure that my safety was maintained. The sad fact is that many of the reported cases of possession that I had to investigate were in lower-income, undeveloped, and poor neighborhoods. He always kept his *khanda*, the ceremonial sword given to him by his father and passed down through his family, alongside him in the front passenger seat. The irony of having a Muslim guard a Catholic was never lost on Mohammed. He always had a great sense of humor, even when traveling through the roughest parts of the city; that was part of his proud warrior heritage. As we arrived at the address and saw my neighbor's cousin in front of the building, Mohammed became unusually somber. As I exited the car, he said something he'd never said before in all the years he worked for me: "Please be careful, Father."

I walked up to the top floor as instructed by the cousin. Before entering, he had informed me that the tenants on that floor had been so frightened of the tenant in 8F that they were all staying with family or others in the building on different floors, leaving the entire floor empty. When I asked why the building's owner hadn't done anything, he looked at me quizzically, as if I should know better. When I reached the floor, none of the hallway lights were working, so I had to use a flashlight from my site visit case in order to find the apartment. The lights within the apartment didn't seem to be working either, with the exception of a glow emanating from the bottom of a closed door at the end of the hallway. The whole apartment smelled rancid, and seemed in complete disarray. The hall carpeting leading to the lighted room was sopping wet. I walked to the end of the hallway, slowly pushed the door open, and was shocked by what I saw.

In sharp contrast to the rest of the apartment, this room was impeccably neat, and smelled as fresh as springtime. On the bed sat a striking man with a powerful build, dressed in dark clothing. He smiled, as if he had anticipated my arrival, and beckoned me toward a chair positioned to the side of the mattress. I sat, removed my notepad, and began my interview. I asked the individual, "Do you know why I'm here?" The man responded, "Of course I do. The real question is, do *you* know why you are here?" He proceeded to ask my denomination, which I confirmed as Roman Catholic. He then asked, "Are you aware of the level of atrocity conducted by your faith throughout history?" For the next several hours, the individual recounted in authoritative detail every major act of violence attributed to the Church for the past several hundred years, from the Crusades to the recent cases of abuse. It was difficult for me to keep up with my note-taking. From those hours, what was clear to me was that this was not a case of demonic possession. The individual before me, however, was also no ordinary human.

When he was finished, I asked him why he was terrorizing the people in this building. "It is you who is the terrorist," he said. "The people in this building, they believe in your faith. Even after all it has done for centuries to cause pain and anguish to your own kind, they follow your words blindly. Your job is to root out evil. What if the source of that evil originates from your faith?" His response shook me to my bones. Not because he made me question my belief; I've had plenty of casual conversations with clever nonbelievers who look to find fault with my convictions. The reason I was afraid was because I realized his intentions. He wasn't hoping I would exorcise him; it was he who wanted to exorcise me. To rattle me enough with his educated and eloquent commentary that I would begin to doubt my faith. What I feared was what would happen if I refused to abandon it.

I stood up from the chair and thanked him for his time. I explained that it was clear that my faith and my services were irrelevant to him, and I would be taking my leave. He leapt up from the bed with astonishing speed, and slammed the door shut. "I'm sorry, Father. It is you who does not understand. If you won't be turned by choice, then you shall be turned by force." He opened the closet door, inside which hung row upon row of clerical garments from various religions—Buddhist, Muslim, and Christian faiths all seemed to be represented, all splattered with varying amounts of gore. I scrambled toward the window, which was cloaked by a heavy curtain, and attempted to force it open. The creature grabbed me by the hair and rammed my head into the wall, causing this wound.

Lavin points to the scar running across his forehead.

PL: It grasped my skull and turned my face upward and sideways, exposing my neck. "Don't worry, Father," he said. "Soon you will realize the extent of your ignorance, and you will wonder why you spent so much of this life wasting it. Fortunately, you will have the rest of eternity to make amends." I felt him bearing down on my neck when suddenly I heard a loud, wet, smacking sound, and my face was splattered with liquid. I turned and saw Mohammed standing behind the creature. Just as the creature was about to feed, Mohammed struck it in the throat with his father's sword. His blow was not powerful enough, and the weapon chopped only halfway through, lodging in the center of the creature's neck.

Choking from the wound, the creature stood and faced Mohammed. With a smile on his face, it whispered, *"Allahu Akbar,"* and twisted its body forcefully to the side with the sword still embedded in its throat. The extended blade sliced Mohammed across his own neck. Choking on his own blood, Mohammed collapsed to the floor, grabbing the creature by the lapels and spitting blood into its face. While it was distracted, I grabbed hold of the back of the sword's blade and forced it the rest of the way through the creature's neck. It made a horrific choking sound as the wound began to heal itself around the weapon, so I twisted the blade back around and cut through the remaining flesh that held its head in place. The creature's skull toppled to the ground, next to Mohammed's body. I fell alongside both, physically spent and mentally exhausted. After regaining some of my strength, I brought both bodies down to the car and departed. After conducting the appropriate research, I disposed of the creature's body.

Mohammed's body was buried according to Muslim tradition, along with his family's sword. In the weeks following, I submitted my resignation to the archdiocese, as well as my request to leave the order.

Vampire Combat Manual: Why did you leave the priesthood?

PL: It was apparent that I was targeted due to my specialized role within the Church. As long as I was privy to that knowledge, I realized that I would be putting not only myself at risk, but the whole archdiocese, if not the entire Vatican. After Mohammed's funeral, I requested a special meeting with senior officials to discuss the incident and share my findings. That request was denied. Repeatedly. The reasoning was that since the incident was not arranged through proper channels, my word would be suspect. My efforts to convince them were unsuccessful. I began to wonder if some of what the creature spoke that night was true.

I soon realized that as much as I would prefer working within the system, it would be better for everyone if I operated as a layman. Since my resignation, I've devoted a great deal of time to tracing the history of this species, as well as monitoring its influence to see if there have been any infiltrations into the clergy.

Lavin takes a long pause before he speaks, as if in contemplation.

PL: Although, I would be lying if I said my conversation that night had nothing to do with my decision. The creature was . . . compelling.

VCM: Have you discovered anything in your studies that would assist others with respect to combat?

Lavin stares at me, as if confused by my inquiry.

PL: I apologize; my memory fails me at times now. What was the nature of your work again?

I explain the project again to Lavin, and hand him a rough draft of my notes that forms the foundation of this manuscript. He excuses himself with the papers and retreats to another room. Several hours pass, and night begins to fall. I am about to take my leave when Lavin returns and sits back down in his chair. He pours himself another drink.

PL: Your work is very thorough.

Based on what I've learned about how this species operates, I foresee one of two consequences should your project actually come to public light. One: They find it mildly amusing and quaint. "A sheep's fantasy of confronting the wolves" as it were, and think nothing more of it. The other consequence: They perceive it as a valid threat to their existence, an act of aggression from our species, and respond accordingly.

VCM: What if it is the latter?
PL: . . . God help us all.

ACKNOWLEDGMENTS

It is tradition on this page to thank those involved in helping the author create his completed work. While a great many individuals deserve my gratitude in relation to this project, I do have some apprehension in expressing it, for the following reason: It is unknown how this work will be received by members of the undead. Based on my experiences researching this project, there is a possibility that retribution will be sought against those who contributed to bringing this information to light. In order to protect my sources and their families from such retaliation, I have decided to abbreviate their surnames or simply keep anonymous all those who assisted me in my work. To those listed, you have my eternal thanks. Stay vigilant.

To Matt W., for still believing.

To Denise S. and Meredith G., for keeping me on track.

To Kurt M., for his talent and professionalism.

To Dr. Benson Y., for the education on anatomy and the emergency room data.

To Dr. Katherine P. for the ancient language translations and the text deciphering.

To Shihan Gene D., Professor Brian G., and my training partners at BBJJ, for making me a better practitioner and student.

To Jimmy B., for the details on raiding operations, room clearing, and firearms.

To those operators who must remain anonymous, your service and your assistance is valued and appreciated.